S0-CBR-063

From the Coup
to the
Commonwealth

From the Coup to the Commonwealth

An Inside Look at Life in Contemporary Russia

Daniel B. Clendenin

Visiting Professor of Christian Studies
Moscow State University, Russia

BAKER BOOK HOUSE
Grand Rapids, Michigan 49516

© 1992 by Daniel B. Clendenin

Published by Baker Book House
P.O. Box 6287, Grand Rapids, Michigan 49516-6287

Printed in the United States of America

All rights reserved. No part of this publication may be reproduced, stored in a retrieval system, or transmitted in any form or by any means—electronic, mechanical, photocopy, recording, or any other—without the prior written permission of the publisher. The only exception is brief quotations within printed reviews.

Library of Congress Cataloging in Publication Data

Clendenin, Daniel B.
    From the coup to the commonwealth : an inside look at life in contemporary Russia / Daniel B. Clendenin.
        p.   cm.
    Includes bibliographical references and index.
    ISBN 0-8010-2574-5
    1. Christianity—Russia (Federation)—History—20th century.
2. Russia (Federation)—Religion. 3. Russia (Federation)—Social conditions.
4. Russia (Federation)—Economic conditions.
5. Americans—Russia (Federation) I. Title.
BR936.C56 1993
209.47—dc20   92-34664

09.47
2593f

L. I. F. E. Bible College
LIBRARY
1100 COVINA BLVD
SAN DIMAS, CA 91773

Contents

0045614

Preface

That we will be crushed, that is the great danger now," Maria Mironova warned. "Communism is gone, the Soviet Union is gone, and everything is falling down around us. It was not that socialism was a good system—it wasn't. It did terrible, terrible things to people. But we do not know that what is coming will be better."

Maria, a math professor and former Communist party member for twenty years, bustled across St. Peterburg's Palace Square behind the magnificent Hermitage Art Museum as winter's early dusk fell and the blowing snow bit into her face. She hurried to purchase bread for her husband and two children before the long queue that had formed bought it all. Like millions of other citizens of the former Soviet Union, she has gladly shed her communist past to support the fledgling democracy movement. Now she wonders where it will all lead. "Everything that has happened is good, for we are finally free of a system that had enslaved us to an ideology that had failed. The Soviet state could not save itself, and the people did not think it worth saving. It died, and I am not mourning. But just how do we get to this new paradise of democracy and full markets? This is where my optimism gives way to a profound pessimism because I doubt that we know the way or will find it easily."[1]

Maria's anxieties recall the dire warning of Alexander Solzhenitsyn, who with prophetic prescience observed eighteen months before Gorbachev's resignation that "time has finally run out for commu-

1. Reported by Michael Parks, *Los Angeles Times*, December 31, 1991, p. H-1.

7

nism. But its edifice has not yet crumbled. May we not be crushed beneath its rubble instead of gaining liberty."[2] As the Soviet edifice continues to disintegrate, the rubble of economic chaos, ethnic strife, dictatorial machinations from both right- and left-wing groups, and widespread civic disillusionment threaten to bury the fragile democratic movement alive. Today the former Soviet Union faces years, even decades, of uncertainty. In his classic analysis of the 1789 revolution that occurred exactly 200 years before the fall of the Berlin Wall in 1989, *The Old Regime and the French Revolution,* Alexis de Tocqueville warned that "for a bad government, the most dangerous time is when it begins to reform itself."[3] Current events in the Commonwealth of Independent States now prove the frightening truth of Tocqueville's dictum. Reform will not come easily or without the possibilities of failure. How should Americans, and indeed the world, respond to this situation?

In the midst of these historical ambiguities and uncertainties, the former Soviet Union needs generous doses of understanding, empathy, and support from the world community if it is to succeed in its efforts to develop a political democracy and a market economy. This book attempts to show how and why that is so. My hope is that it will heighten the understanding and deepen the empathy and concern of Americans toward a great nation and people who now face a future that is uncertain, fraught with peril, and perhaps even foreboding. We have not always done a good job at either understanding or empathy.

Our understanding has been obscured by stereotypes that have portrayed the former Soviet Union as a mysterious and closed society. Sir Winston Churchill's aphorism of October 1, 1939, that the Soviet Union was "a riddle wrapped in a mystery inside an enigma," characterizes the attitude of many people in the West even today. Of course there are reasons for this and at least a portion of truth in the stereotype; until very recently Russia *has* been a closed society sometimes characterized by historical ambivalence and even xenophobia toward the West. One could even plot the ebb and flow of

2. Alexander Solzhenitsyn, "Rebuilding Russia," July 1990.
3. Alexis de Tocqueville, *The Old Regime and the French Revolution* (New York: Harper, 1856), p. 214.

that cultural ambivalence, beginning with the early tsars' alternating hostility (Ivan the Terrible) and openness (Peter the Great, Catherine the Great) toward the West. But more recent and explicit xenophobia has been the product of calculated state manipulation of its citizens; it hardly reflects the truth about the Russian people themselves. Further, the Commonwealth of Independent States is no longer closed. The "iron curtain" (a phrase coined by Churchill in a March 5, 1946 speech in Fulton, Missouri) which had been lowered from the Baltic to the Adriatic has been rent, and today an entire expatriate community (estimated at 80,000 for Moscow alone) of students, scholars, businesspeople, and Christian workers now lives in this formerly closed country. This book might be seen as an early press release about an unfolding drama that is still in its earliest stages, with the hope that increased understanding will replace misguided stereotypes.

Nor have we Americans been very empathetic toward Russia. Too many of us have been blinded by the rhetoric that Russia was "an evil empire" and America's archenemy. True, there are reasons for this stereotype, too, and no one with any knowledge of Soviet history would ever discount the Soviet Union's past expansionist aggression and its hostile military ambitions. Anyone who doubts those facts should read the monumental and disturbing work by Mikhail Heller and Aleksandr Nekrich, *Utopia in Power*. The failed war in Afghanistan, which left 1 million dead, 2 million disabled, and 5 million refugees (the largest refugee population in the world), is only the most recent example of a clear pattern. But times have changed and this is no longer true either. The cold war is over. While Reagan used the saber rattle to fulfill his presidential ambitions, Bush sought to play the peace dividend. Former bastions of communist influence like Cuba and North Korea (the latter of which invited evangelist Billy Graham to visit in April 1992) struggle for new forms of existence now that Moscow no longer fills their coffers and kitchens. The largest nation on earth (geographically speaking) has been humbled and brought to its knees. The currents of democracy that swept across Eastern Europe in 1989 hit the Russian Empire with the destructive force of a tidal wave. The former Soviet Union and its former republics need and deserve our empathy and help, not our scorn or apathy. (What shape this help should take is a different and complicated question.) From a Christian perspective, too, it seems strange to consider any nation an "enemy," especially one like Russia, which long before America ever existed, and only until recent years, was by design and intent a Christian civilization. I have often pondered how the beautiful architecture of Russian churches, some of which date back to the fourteenth and fifteenth centuries, has been a silent but constant witness to this fact during the last seventy-five years. Among all peoples, Christians especially should be people of empathy.

If this book can help to foster greater understanding and deeper empathy I will be grateful. In that sense it is a call to care. Both understanding and empathy are needed. The former without the latter is arid and lifeless; empathy without knowledge is misguided. Together, understanding and empathy can offer realistic help to a good people in great need.

For convenience I have organized my thoughts around four themes. After a short introduction to my family's life and work in the former Soviet Union, and a chapter outlining my first impressions about life in Russia, I examine the three realms of economics, politics, and religion.

It is my pleasure to thank the many people, both American and Soviet, who have enriched our lives through supporting us in a myriad of ways during our stay in Moscow: Daryl McCarthy, executive director of the International Institute for Christian Studies; our staff—Marsha Wilson, Delores Cole, Dana Preusch, and Brent Hulett; the IICS board of directors; fellow IICS professors Bob Young and Sharon Linzey; our many friends at our home church in Farmington Hills, Michigan, Grace Chapel EPC; Vladimir Dobrenkov, Alexander Panin, Igor Yablakov, Alexander Krasnikov, Alexander Popov, Vasily Vasilovich Golubev, and Anton Petrenko of Moscow State University; Mikhail Selamaten, Ira Vishik, Alexander and Irena Kargin, Andrei and Olga Fillipov, and Maria Gotsiridre of Moscow; Ben Fairfax and Paul and Mary Wohlers of the American Embassy in Moscow; Lena Spirkina, Tatyana Shevelenkova, and Galena Chentsova of the Russian Academy of Science's Institute of Psychology; Igor Fillipov, director of the Lenin Library; Mamedov Bakhtiar Nariman and his family of Azerbaijan; Oleg Kolobov of Nizhni Novgorod State University; Valery Oryol of

Yaroslavl State University; Vitaly Tselishchev of Novosibirsk State University; Yuri and Natalia Salonin, and Anna Tipseena of St. Petersburg State University; Constantine Ivanov of the Society for Open Christianity in St. Petersburg; Marat, Elias, and Aysa Kasanov of the University of Kazakhstan, and Sergei Popov, all from Alma-Ata; Maja Kuhle and Janis Vejs of the Institute of Philosophy of the Latvian Academy of Science in Riga; Juris Rosenvalds of the University of Latvia; Victor, Lucia, and Cyril Molchanov of Rostov on Don State University; Victor and Genia Rebalchinka of Vilnius; Jakavonyte-Gavrilenkiene Laimute of the Lithuanian Conservatory in Vilnius; our community of Christian friends in Moscow—Andrew Buckler, Serge and Donna Duss, Peter and Anita Deyneka, Teri Hodges, Orest and Susan Holavaty, Kent and Janice Hill, Ray and Cindy LeClair, John and Barbara Melin, Mark and Valeri Powers, Ken and Laurel Wrye, and Priscilla Young; my editors from Baker Book House, Jim Weaver and Maria denBoer; and family and friends who have lent special help of various sorts—Lud and Trudy Koci, Roger and Mary Simpson, Bob and Christina Swanson, Phil and Nancy Payne, Phil and Rachel Rohrer, Dan and Dori Penning, Tony and Jan DeOrio, Ken and Diane Graves, Chuck and Beth Viane, James and Dorothy Wood, Voravit and Joanna Ratanatharathorn, Jon Huegli, Jim and Sharon Heimbach, and John and Madelle Payne.

I would like to dedicate this book to my wife, Patty, who more than once was rightly called a "hero" by our Russian friends; and to our three children, Matthew, Andrew, and Megan, with the hope that it will help all of us to cherish the wonderful memories of our time together in the former Soviet Union.

Daniel B. Clendenin
Moscow
August 1992

1

A Society at Sea

To unknown shores, must be our cry, fearless through
the storms, on, past all the shallows. . . . On to new
shores, there is no turning back.

—M. Mussorgsky
Letters from 1972,
1875[1]

Advent of an Adventure

The Coup That Failed

Just days before our scheduled departure, the Monday morning
phone call startled my wife and me. It was barely 7 A.M., and the
children were still sleeping. Who would call at such an early hour?
Phone calls at that time usually portend something unusual, perhaps even some unwanted news. I picked up the receiver to hear
our neighbor ask, "Is your TV on?" Her question remained a family

1. O. von Rieseman, *Moussorgsky* (New York, 1929), pp. 105, 248.

joke, for our television was rarely on, much less at 7 o'clock in the morning. But the phone call was no joke. "A coup has ousted Gorbachev! I told you that you shouldn't go!" Our minds reeled. The unthinkable had happened. How could it be? Months of extensive planning for our family's two-year trip to Moscow State University seemed to evaporate with that single phone call. How could we ever go to the Soviet Union now? Feelings of helplessness, despair, and frustration swept over us. Our dozens of attempts to phone Moscow, of course, failed.

Morning news services began to piece together the sketchy information. Gennady Yanayev, an ethnic Russian, had led a right-wing conservative coup that seized power from Gorbachev while he vacationed with his family in the Crimea. Typical foggy rhetoric that Westerners have come to expect from Soviet officialdom declared that Gorbachev was unable to fulfill his duties due to "health reasons." His whereabouts were unknown, and some reports indicated he was under house arrest. When appointed to his vice-presidential post, Yanayev had declared himself to be "a communist to the depths of my soul." Reform-minded liberals had interpreted his appointment to the vice presidency by Gorbachev as yet another dangerous concession to hard-liners resistant to change. Later he would take blame for a coup by his own confidants. They were right. Pledging to take "decisive measures" to end the country's crisis, the eight archconservative hard-liners, including Interior Minister Boris Pugo, Defense Minister Dmitri Yazov, and KGB chief Vladimir Kryuchkov, appointed themselves as a state committee to run the country under the declared "state of emergency." In the same breath they insisted that their emergency measures "in no way indicated a refusal from the course of deep reforms in all spheres of life, state and society." But their actions belied their words as tanks rumbled through the streets of Moscow and all but one television station was cut off. The Russian White House, adjacent to the American Embassy, became the focus of the coup as a crude blockade was formed to protect Yeltsin from the troops. Gorbachev and Yeltsin were silent. The committee of eight declared that federal laws had "unconditional priority" throughout the USSR, and, more ominous still, that any groups that spread "moral and physical terror" would be liquidated. News bulletins changed hourly. President Bush called the developments "murky" and "disturbing." Yanayev and TASS declared that Gorbachev was undergoing medical treatment and that they looked forward to his return. Yeltsin eventually called for civil disobedience and urged the people not to go to work.

As I contemplated how quickly our months of planning had come unglued, I was reminded of several scriptural passages that declare the sovereignty of God over the sovereignties of nations—"The LORD has made everything for its own purpose, even the wicked for the day of evil" (Prov. 16:4); "The King's heart is like channels of water in the hand of the LORD; he turns it wherever He wishes" (Prov. 21:1)—and the tentative nature of all human plans and pretensions— "Now listen, you who say, 'Today or tomorrow we will go to this or that city, spend a year there, carry on business and make money.' Why, you do not even know what will happen tomorrow. What is your life? You are a mist that appears for a little while and then vanishes. Instead, you ought to say, 'If it is the Lord's will, we will live and do this or that'" (James 4:13–16).

In the end the coup turned out to be little more than a farce by ill-organized and incompetent party hacks. In three short days it was over. Pugo shot his wife and then committed suicide; thirteen others are now in prison and await trial. Like many Americans, I listened with fascination to the live radio press conference as Gorbachev, back in Moscow, recounted the unfolding drama of those three days at the Crimea. His cadence was slow and deliberate as he narrated exact details, at times pausing to gather his emotions. Later it became a cynical joke in Moscow that the president had more time to write a book about the coup for hard-currency royalties than to do anything of lasting import about the country's crisis that he himself had precipitated.[2]

In another sense, however, the coup was not a farce but a pivotal turning point. It accelerated the momentum of cataclysmic change that from that time forward seemed to take on a life of its own and signaled the point of no return toward radical economic and political reforms. It represented the last gasp of a dying hard-line communism in Moscow. Gorbachev resigned as president of the Com-

2. Mikhail Gorbachev, *The August Coup* (San Francisco: Harper Collins, 1991).

munist party; Yeltsin banned the Party from Russia altogether (it had lost 4 million members in the previous five years). Statues of communist saints throughout the city literally toppled, including one of Felix Dzerzhinski, founder of the KGB. Many of these fallen saints were piled in Moscow's so-called park of fallen idols. Other monuments, especially those of Lenin like the one beside our apartment building, were defaced with fresh grafitti (an otherwise uncommon phenomenon in Moscow, unlike in major American cities). A month later the KGB was dissolved. Street and subway station names changed, including those like Prospect Marx, the oldest metro stop of the entire system (built around 1935). City names reverted to their pre-Revolutionary designations: Leningrad became St. Petersburg, and Gorky became Nizhni Novgorod. The three Baltic states declared their independence and were immediately granted diplomatic recognition by Western nations. Within weeks all twelve remaining republics made similar declarations of autonomy. By early September 1991 Radio News Moscow was already referring to "the former Soviet Union." *Pravda,* whose circulation had fallen from 10 million to 500,000, was shut down (since then it resumed publication, only to be shut down a second time). The *World Marxist Review,* which had been founded in 1958 and was distributed to 145 nations in 37 languages, ceased publication. The first week of November 1991, for the first time since 1917, the annual Red Square parade of military hardware that commemorated the Bolshevik Revolution was discontinued. By mid-December the Soviet Bank of Foreign Economic Relations (*Vnesheconombank*), saddled with $80 billion of foreign debt, was declared bankrupt. More than 80 Soviet government ministries shut down, putting 50,000 people out of work.

More significant, the coup marked a definitive beginning of the end for Gorbachev himself, who could never quite stay ahead of the crushing wave of reform he himself had initiated when he took office almost six years earlier. In a few months the "new thinking" of perestroika (the subtitle of his own book) would sweep him aside with astonishing speed and little more to show for it than ego-bruising opinion polls. Gorbachev had always been much more popular abroad than among his own people; an October 1991 opinion poll in Novosibirsk found that 82 percent of those polled were against

Gorbachev staying in power. His extensive efforts to maintain a Union Treaty, a strategy he urged even long after his resignation, were an embarrassing failure and a graphic example of his loss of power. Half of the twelve remaining republics no longer even attended sessions of the Soviet parliament. Following summits at Minsk and Alma-Ata, the presidents of Russia, Ukraine, and Byelorussia (Boris Yeltsin, Leonid Kravchuk, and Stanislav Shushkevich; Gorbachev was not invited) unilaterally pronounced the dissolution of the Soviet regime and the formation of the Commonwealth of Independent States. Long unwilling to concede defeat, in a two-hour press conference on December 12, 1991 Gorbachev hinted at the inevitable: "The main work of my life is done. I have done all that I could. I think that in my place others would have long ago given up, but I have managed to drag through, if not without mistakes, the main ideas of perestroika." Three days later he reversed his posture and insisted that he would not resign. But the end was at hand. At 7:30 P.M. in Moscow on December 25, 1991, just four months after the failed coup and to the surprise of no one, Gorbachev read his rather anticlimactic, twelve-minute resignation speech (see Appendix A for the complete text). I will never forget that evening, as it was Christmas Day (for Westerners, not Russians), and we were celebrating with good friends at the American Embassy. We were glued to the television as CNN carried the event live. Although the speech was little more than a formality at that point, Gorbachev was defiant to the very end. He complained that the actions of Yeltsin, Kravchuk, and Shushkevich were totally undemocratic, that the issue of the union of the fifteen republics should be decided by a vote of the people, and that Yeltsin and his cohorts had "carved up the country like a pie." As if to add insult to injury, and indicative of Muscovites' weariness with politics and preoccupation with surviving the harsh winter, in Moscow Gorbachev's resignation passed almost without notice. A day later the Soviet parliament voted itself out of existence. The red Soviet flag with the yellow hammer and sickle was lowered from atop the Kremlin for the last time and replaced with the Russian Republic flag of red, white, and blue. A vast empire of 300 million people had vanished, with precious little idea what would take its place.

Conversely, the coup also insured the final rise to power of Boris Yeltsin and granted him the mandate he had sought since being elected president of the Russian Republic only months earlier. Images of him defiantly mounting the tanks at the barricades in front of the Russian White House during the coup to urge the people to take to the streets to defend democracy (which several hundred thousand did) are still etched in the minds of many. Yet he faces an almost impossible task: He must not only rebuild a shattered economy but restore the very political fabric of a land of 300 million people and over 100 ethnolinguistic groups. Most Muscovites do not like him any more than they did Gorbachev, primarily because of his unrelenting path of radical economic reform. They consider him an autocratic demagogue who, even more than Gorbachev, is marching them pell mell off the cliff into economic chaos. One thing is certain: He has committed himself to a path of radical reform and shock therapy toward a genuine market economy. On January 2, 1992, he ignored widespread hostilities and lifted state controls on prices that had kept consumer prices artificially low for decades. As expected, prices on all products soared. The price of bread increased sixfold, from 40 kopecks to more than 2 rubles (and, as I write today, a loaf of bread now costs 12 rubles—a thirtyfold increase or 3000 percent inflation in one year); a bottle of vodka that sold for 10 rubles now costs 45 (a day's wages). Many of the state stores, unsure of what all of the changes meant, did not even open for several days after the Christmas holidays. Others were open, but as usual had nothing to sell. When I asked a friend of mine if he had noticed the price increases, he observed that it was hard to tell because the stores were empty. Whether a political democracy and a free market economy can survive their neonatal condition and move on to a pattern of growth and maturity remains to be seen. As one editorial put it, the irony of the August coup was that the people defended democracy before they had built it.

In fact, although the coup did represent a bold defense of nascent democracy, in a way it has led many people to resent perestroika due to the phenomenon of unfulfilled expectations. Mariya Remizova, defender of the White House who manned the barricades of democracy for the three days of the coup, put it this way: "Soon I realized that not much had changed except for the removal of

Dzerzhinski's monument. It is easier for the politicians to speak than to do." Some people thought the coup would usher in dramatic improvements. Optimistic expectations for improved living conditions after ousting the communists were in fact met with just the opposite—rapidly deteriorating conditions. As the harsh winter descended on Moscow, food lines grew longer, layoffs increased, prices skyrocketed, and the value of the ruble plummeted. "Nothing has changed for the better. Nothing. It's a great pity to stand in line and watch life get worse," observed Alexander Averkin. Whether Muscovites will consider freedom of speech, press, and the political process worth the price of short-term economic collapse remains to be seen. Will the coup continue to symbolize the march toward democracy, or will it backfire and provoke a return to the past? Only the future will tell.[3]

A week after the coup a friend of mine joked that I would travel to the USSR but that I would return home from a new nation. Little did he know how prophetic he was. The federal government that existed for seventy-five years is gone; the land and its people remain, drifting in a sea of change with no apparent rudder. In Mussorgsky's metaphor from 100 years earlier, the former Soviet Union searches for new shores, but is not at all certain how to get there.

From Detroit to Moscow

Our home was rented, and literally echoed because it was so empty; everything we owned had either been sold, packed into boxes and suitcases, or put into storage. Outside, change was in the air. Autumn announced its presence with the Labor Day weekend; the leaves from the old ash trees in our front yard rained down at a 45 degree angle (never straight down). A massive thunderstorm made our final days in Detroit gray and gloomy. With the coup over, only a few final details separated us from our departure for Moscow State University, where I would assume a two-year appointment as a guest professor in Christian Studies: a final phone call to Moscow verifying my arrival; a visit by a Russian Jewish friend who gave our 8-week-old

---

3. Quotations taken from "The Big Letdown," *Moscow Guardian*, October 18, 1991, pp. 1, 3. Hereafter cited as *MG*.

baby girl a darling matryoska doll, along with phone numbers of
family and friends in Moscow for Patty and me; a special day of worship at Church of the Madonna in inner-city Detroit as guests of
dear friends, followed by lunch at a favorite restaurant in Greek-
town; church friends who stopped by our home late our last evening
to help us with final packing and to pray; and last-minute good-byes
to family and friends.

"Everything is under control!" Anna assured me in her heavy
Russian accent on the telephone from Zig-Zag Travel in New York.
Like our neighbor's Monday morning phone call, her comment and
the name of her travel agency have remained family jokes. Our
domestic plane tickets for the flight from Detroit to New York would
arrive only a day or two before we were to leave. Anna would hand
deliver our visas and international tickets in transit, between flights at
JFK. There were only two problems: Our flight from Detroit to
New York departed at 6 A.M., meaning we would have to rise at 3
A.M. in order to leave for the airport at 4 A.M.; and our visas were
good for only 10 days. Didn't Anna know what it was like to travel
with three young children?! Didn't she know I intended to be gone
for two years, not two weeks?! Trying to put a humorous spin on
it all, I recalled a Swahili phrase we saw on a T-shirt the previous
summer in Nairobi, *hakunnah matatah*, which might be roughly
translated into American idiom as, "not to worry!"

Wednesday morning we awoke in the middle of the night, piled
our three groggy children into the borrowed van that we had finished loading only a few hours earlier, and pulled out of the driveway.
How strange it was to leave behind six years of friends, relation-
ships, and precious memories in our first house. Patty's brother and
family met us at the airport to help us process our twenty-seven
boxes of household goods ($2,600 in excess baggage). We had taken
seriously the advice that whatever you thought you might possibly
need in Russia you should take with you.

Good friends from Flushing met us when we landed at JFK at
8:30 A.M., and Patty and the kids left with them for a day of fun in
the city. I remained behind at the Aeroflot check-in counter to guard
our twenty-seven boxes until the late afternoon flight to Moscow.
Even there in the terminal my Russian education began, as I enjoyed

a conversation with Natasha, a student at Moscow State where I would be teaching.

"Everything is under control!" said Anna, but this time to a group of perhaps 100 or more Hasidic Jews who were booked on our flight. Replete in their black garb from head to foot, their long sidelocks dangling from their heads, the mostly male group talked boisterously on the long flight from New York to Moscow, as if they were the only ones aboard. I found their sense of joy, community, and spontaneity to be infectious, and a welcome relief from the long monotony and mindless movies typical of my previous international flights. Before takeoff and landing they donned their phylacteries. In midflight they swayed to and fro as they read their sacred scriptures. They locked arms and danced and sang up and down the aisles of the plane in mid-flight, and again at the luggage carousel in Moscow's Sheremetyevo airport, as if to hasten the arrival of their baggage.

Our youngest son Andrew slept for ten straight hours, from takeoff in New York to landing in Moscow. Matthew, our oldest, became airsick, just as he had on our flight to Frankfurt a year earlier. Baby Megan, only eight weeks old, seemed oblivious to it all. Our routing took us over Greenland and Iceland, across Norway, Sweden, and Finland, and on into Moscow. Two hours after landing we finally retrieved our twenty-seven boxes and cleared customs with only one of them sent through the x-ray machine. As we pushed our way through the crowded terminal to the exits, what a welcome sight it was to see Professor Alexander Krasnikov of the university waiting for us. He had obtained an ancient university clunker of a bus to take us to the university where we would live and work. At long last, and in spite of the coup and Zig Zag Travel, we were in Moscow.

Overview of the Former Soviet Union, Moscow, and MSU

The Former Soviet Union

Although the Soviet Union itself no longer exists in a formal sense, a fact that is still slow to register in my mind and hard to believe when it does, its peoples and republics certainly do in a material sense. Almost no one doubts that the fragile commonwealth of eleven states will occupy center stage in the world's geopolitics for decades to come and demand the best minds that we have. In his interview with CNN immediately after his resignation speech, Gorbachev referred to the enormous size and ethnic complexity of the former empire as one of the factors that contributed to its eventual disintegration.

With Scandinavian beginnings among a Slavic people in the Kievan forests sometime around the middle of the eighth century, at the time of its recent dissolution the Union of Soviet Socialist Republics (USSR) was the largest nation in the world. Stretching from the Alaskan peninsula in the east, where it is separated from American territory by only a few miles of the Bering Strait, to Central Europe in the west, the country spanned eleven time zones and nearly 7,000 miles (2.5 times larger than the United States). From north to south it measured 3,500 miles. In terms of population, its nearly 300 million people ranked it third in the world, behind China and India and just ahead of the United States. Although half of the population is ethnic Russian, some 120 ethnolinguistic groups (eighteen of which have more than a million speakers) provided the tinder for the fires of nationalism that ignited from Gorbachev's policies of glasnost and perestroika. Put another way, half of the people in the former Soviet Union are not Russian. A land enormously rich in natural resources, even at the time of its dissolution in 1991 the USSR was the world's largest oil producer. The fifteen republics have 65 percent of the world's natural gas reserves, more than all of the Middle East combined. Its coal comprises over 50 percent of world reserves. Soviet timber and manganese resources are the largest in the world. Its production of gold and platinum ranks second only to South Africa's.

Moscow

A popular Russian proverb says that Kiev is the mother of Russia but Moscow is its heart (and St. Petersburg its head). The first reference to the capital of the USSR[4] is contained in the Chronicle of Ipatyev, written around the middle of the twelfth century. The first

---

4. Moscow has always been the capital of Russia except for the period 1712–1918, when Peter the Great moved the capital to St. Petersburg. In March 1918, Lenin moved the capital back to Moscow.

wooden Kremlin fortress dates to the year 1156, built by Prince Yuri Dolgoruky, and from then until now it has formed the nucleus of the city. Today one can still visit the magnificent sixteenth-century cathedrals within its walls and see the crypts of rulers dating back to the first decades of the fifteenth century. Like a secular saint to whom people still pay hommage on a mecca, Lenin's embalmed body rests in the center of Red Square in the somber, dark red granite mausoleum erected in 1930. Behind the mausoleum and adjacent to the massive Kremlin wall are the tombs of dozens of prominent Soviet leaders, including Lenin's wife, Stalin, and Brezhnev. Today Moscow is a city of some 10 million people and still the political, cultural, transportation, and intellectual center of the former country.

Moscow State University

At the north end of Red Square stands the current history museum, the oldest in Moscow, which in fact was originally the first site of Moscow State University. Founded in 1755 and named after Mikhail Lomonosov, the greatest figure of Russia's Enlightenment, today the university is spread across the city, although its primary campus is in the southwest part of town in an imposing secular cathedral built by Stalin with prison labor from 1949 to 1953. Rising twenty-nine stories, from which one gains a breath-taking panorama of the entire city, its wedding-cake architecture is a mass of marble, granite, and wooden parque floors. The most prestigious and competitive of Moscow's 80 institutes and universities of higher education, MSU is not only the oldest but the largest university in the former country. It boasts some 17 faculties or schools that are subdivided into nearly 300 departments or chairs, a faculty of 3,000, a student body of 30,000, and Gorky Library with more than 6 million volumes (complemented by the Lenin Library in the center of the city, by one measure the largest library in the world with 40 million volumes). Tuition is free to the students, and they receive a monthly living stipend of about 500 rubles.

A New Appointment

In February 1991 I joined millions of other Americans in the unemployment line, but as God would have it, the following spring I was thrilled to accept a two-year appointment to Moscow State through the International Institute for Christian Studies of Overland Park, Kansas, which had negotiated a two-year contract with the university to provide a professor of Christian studies.[5] My appointment was to the faculty of philosophy in the Department of the History and Theory of Religion and Freethinking, roughly similar to what Westerners would call the Department of the Philosophy of Religion. While a university of this size always entertains guest lecturers from abroad, I found it fascinating to contemplate the wonder of being perhaps the first full-time evangelical professor for the next two years in what only a few years earlier was called the Department of Scientific Atheism. While American universities remain paralyzed by political correctness and liberal closedmindedness, I have always thought that it was to its credit that Moscow University was willing to admit and cast aside its ideological blinders of the last seven decades. When IICS presented a Christian Research Library Collection of nearly 1,000 books to the university, both the dean of the philosophy faculty and vice rector of the university remarked to me how much they appreciated the books because they would help their students and faculty move beyond decades of "parochialism" (their word). What a paradoxical thought: to realize that here in the former bastion of Marxist atheism I was doing something I could almost certainly not do in a public university in America—teach Christian studies from an evangelical perspective. In lecture opportunities at other Soviet universities (in Nizhni-Novgorod, Rostov, Riga, St. Petersburg, Novosibirsk, and Azerbaijan), a local Moscow high school, Moscow State's philological faculty, and a group of Muscovite psychologists, I have never encountered anything but unfailing courtesy, enormous kindness beyond what I deserved, and openness to what for some were very new ways of thinking. Never once did I encounter any ideological restrictions whatsoever. The university paid me for my work, giving me a salary of 700 rubles a month (about $10 a month when I first started, but only about half that amount now), more than many professors and twice what the average citizen made. As a point of comparison, months after Yeltsin lifted price controls, a physician

5. IICS now has contracts with about two dozen universities in the former Soviet Union.

friend of mine in Baku, Azerbaijan still makes 400 rubles a month.
Housing, always in short supply in Moscow, was likewise provided.
Spartan by Western standards, our 250 square feet for a family of
five in two dorm rooms was commodious by local standards. As one
student remarked to us when he learned where we lived: "conditions
there are very nice!"

To my surprise, the dean wanted me to lecture in English. Of
course this made the lecture material simpler, but he was eager for
the students to practice English. During the fall semester of 1991 I
offered two courses considered compulsory by our department chair:
a lecture on the Christian worldview, and a seminar in which participants conducted a critical reading of *Mere Christianity* by C. S.
Lewis (translated into Russian by the Slavic Gospel Association).
My students were a combination of graduate and upper level under-
graduates. At the end of my first semester several of them wanted
to continue our deliberations beyond the classroom, a pleasure we
indulged at a weekly lunch at a Georgian cafe near the Park Kul-
tury metro station. For the second semester I offered a course on
contemporary American theology. In addition, since the early fall
of 1991 I have lectured once a week on the Book of Romans to a
group of a dozen psychologists and psychiatrists.

Beyond Socialism

As the former Soviet Union sails uncharted waters and navigates
a socialist command economy toward a supply-demand market economy, and a political dictatorship toward a participatory democracy, it
faces numerous and complex challenges. To understand the nature of
their journey, in the following chapters we will look at the shoals of
economics, politics, and religion that they must negotiate. Before
that, however, we must appreciate the very mundane but important
frustrations and joys of everyday life that the average Soviet citizen
faces. To that we now turn.

2

Five First Impressions

Paradoxes of Soviet Life:
(1) There's no unemployment, but no one works; (2) no one works but productivity goes up; (3) productivity goes up, but there's nothing in the stores; (4) there's nothing in the stores, but at home there's everything; (5) at home there's everything, but no one is satisfied; (6) no one is satisfied, but everyone votes yes.

—Soviet Underground Humor[1]

Introduction

Before moving on to the specifics of economics, politics, and religion, it will prove helpful to record some general impressions about Soviet society, its people, and the paradoxical fate they now face. My impressions derive from two primary sources: my everyday experiences of life and work here (friendships, conversations, teaching, shopping, taxi rides, travel, my journal, and so on) and reflections

1. Cited by Vadim Medish, *The Soviet Union*, 4th ed. (Englewood Cliffs, N.J.: Prentice-Hall, 1991), p. 329.

about them; and reading in the local press. These initial impressions will then serve as a Gestalt of sorts for the chapters that follow.

First impressions are risky, and can be incorrect, and generalizations about an entire people are hazardous, especially when made by a newcomer or outsider. Barriers of language and culture often stymie communication, nuance, and understanding, so that missiologists rightly warn us that what sometimes occurs is projection rather than induction or deduction. My previous travels in Europe, Asia, and Africa have sensitized me to this in sometimes painful and embarrassing ways. Nevertheless, outsiders or newcomers can enjoy certain advantages. Standing "outside" their host culture, they can be sensitive to patterns of life that are so ingrained, habitual, and second-nature to natives that the latter never notice them. I am sure my reader has experienced this phenomenon when interacting with expatriates living in America. They sometimes make observations about American life and culture that are unusually perceptive, insights that perhaps we have never thought about before. In fact, one benefit of these cross-cultural dynamics is that we have an unusually good opportunity to learn about our own cultural background and how it has formed our self-identity. I like how a friend of mine who has traveled in nearly 100 countries put it when he said that living cross-culturally helped him to learn how much of his identity was truly Christian and how much of it was merely American. Further, we can recall how literary precedents by the newcomer/outsider have enriched us. Tocqueville was an outsider to America, but he is still acknowledged today as an astute and perceptive observer of our nation, its life, and its people. The German theologian Helmut Thielicke has left us interesting reflections about his sojourn in Africa. In his important study *The Russian Religious Mind*, George Fedotov notes that Russian observers of their own country are often hampered by "nearness and habit . . . partiality and preconceptions," and that to a certain degree foreigners enjoy some advantages over nationals in studying Russia.[2]

In my own mind I do not think I traveled to the former Soviet Union with many, if any, preconceived ideas or expectations. From the

---

2. George Fedotov, *The Russian Religious Mind* (New York: Harper Torchbooks, 1965), pp. xiii–xiv.

perspective of politics and economics I entertain no ideological pre-commitments to the right or the left. Finally, I have been encour-aged by friends, both Russian and expatriates, people who know Soviet society far better than I do and who were kind enough to cri-tique my thoughts before this book was published, that what follows is accurate. I would even say that I am being too cautious and apolo-getic. What follows is hardly controversial, complex, or erudite; for most people who live in Moscow and the former Soviet republics the following five observations are little more than truisms, in some instances tragic ones, of everyday life in a society at sea. In the final chapter of his cultural history of Russia, *The Icon and the Axe,* James Billington employs the concepts of irony and paradox to capture the essence of Russian life and history. Likewise, the following five obser-vations speak to the pain and the beauty, the grandeur and the misery, of contemporary life in the former Soviet Union.

The East Looks West: Love and Ignorance

Admiration

Before we traveled to the former Soviet Union, a question entered our minds. If only a few years ago Americans stigmatized the Soviet Union as the "evil empire" and a nation of atheists (presumably far worse than our own "secular humanists"!), we wondered how Sovi-ets would see Americans. Would they return the favor of a vicious stereotype and see America as the "great satan" as Kohmeni did? Would they spurn us? Would we be able to make friends? It was hard to answer these questions in advance because so few Western-ers had lived in the Soviet Union for an extended period of time. But having lived here for over a year now the answer is very clear indeed. Most Russians love Americans.

After Sunday worship at the Protestant Chaplaincy of Moscow, a group of American friends would regularly enjoy dinner at the Sputnik Hotel on Leninsky Prospect, just down the street from our place of worship. It was one of the few places we had found that would take a group of a dozen people with kids with no advance reservation. Like most public buildings in Moscow, the hotel had a large coat-check that received heavy use during the long, cold winters. One Sunday our group bustled out of the vicious cold and into the lobby. We removed our coats, and as I gave them to the two elderly, gruff-looking men behind the counter, one of them asked if we were Italians. Glad for the opportunity to practice the simple Russian phrases I had been learning, I responded that no, we were not Italian but "Amerikantsky." The man's face broke into a spontaneous ear-to-ear, toothless grin. He grabbed my hand and pumped it with an exaggerated handshake, exclaiming, "Ah, Americans! Good!" They proceeded to give my two boys pieces of candy. Such displays of emotion are rare in Soviet society; it was a graphic example of how high America's stock is in the former Soviet Union.

In a land of icons that treasures the aesthetic and visual above the analytical and cognitive, one of the greatest examples of Moscow's love affair with America is the West's paradigmatic icon, the golden arches of McDonald's that rise on Gorky Street at Pushkin Square near the center of the city about a mile from the Kremlin. Opened in 1990 as a cooperative venture between McDonald's of Canada and the Soviet Union, the restaurant is the first of a plan that at one time called for the Chicago-based chain to open a dozen restaurants in the capital city. Today it struggles with Moscow's bureaucracy to open a second one on the Arbat. As the largest McDonald's in the world (before the Beijing location opened in the spring of 1992), the Moscow restaurant incarnates the American ideals that bigger is better and efficiency a necessity. With four floors and a seating capacity for 900 people, at any given time the restaurant is thronged with 1,200 to 1,300 people. Two hundred bright, well-trained Russian workers, in uniforms and caps immediately recognizable to American visitors, scurry behind the counter in a frenzy of controlled chaos and efficiency. Floors are constantly mopped and cleaned of winter slush, bathrooms sparkle, workers greet customers when they enter and leave, tables are cleared and wiped immediately after customers finish and rise to leave (a necessity at any rate because more often than not people are waiting around your table with full trays in hand). No wonder that by the fall of 1991 the restaurant was serving 50,000 people a day, a deluge that had become so counter-productive for McDonald's that in November and December of 1991 the restaurant doubled its prices twice in six weeks in order to cut down the traffic to 30,000 a day (increases in its costs of meat, flour, and potatoes also contributed to the price hikes). People were buying large numbers of hamburgers not only to eat on the premises but to take home and freeze, a fact my second-grade son attests to based on his classmates' lunch boxes! On Friday nights it was not unusual for the line to snake some 500 yards around all four sides of Pushkin Square, causing a Russian friend of mine to observe wryly that he had not been to McDonald's because, far from serving fast food, it took hours to get in. Security guards help to control the pushing and shoving of potentially rowdy crowds. At least a half-dozen price hikes have reduced some of the throngs; they also illustrate the hyperinflation that plagues the current economy and evokes the wrath of its citizens. Today, the cost of a "Beeg Mok" attack will set back a Soviet citizen the equivalent of three days' wages. Since opening barely two years ago, the price of a Big Mac has increased 2,000 percent, from 3.75 rubles to nearly 80 rubles. Add Coke and fries and the total is almost a week's wages.[3] But people continue to come, and not only to McDonald's but to the two other Western food chains in Moscow right now, Pizza Hut, with lines that rival those at McDonald's, and Baskin-Robbins ice cream (each with two Moscow locations).

Ignorance

In my travels to nearly a dozen cities in five former republics, I have never experienced anything but warmth and acceptance as an American. People seem to have a natural curiosity and eagerness to learn about the land they have heard about but had hidden from them for so long by the state-controlled media. Sometimes their ignorance takes a funny turn that throws one into a time warp, as when after one lecture a student stood up and asked me about the current status of the Woodstock people in America. This Soviet interest in America has also engendered a sort of wide-eyed naivete that can be both humorous and frustrating. For example, many Soviets simply have no concept of the value of money and the relationship of

---

3. Here and in the remainder of this book, all financial figures were accurate at the time of writing. As Russia's economic reforms continue these figures will become outdated.

money to goods and services rendered or received. One cab driver once asked me for $50 for a ride that was worth little more than a dollar. The interesting point is that he was not trying to rip me off; based on our conversation he knew that I was an American, without doubt very rich, and he figured I could and would easily pay such a price. When I balked, he asked for $20. When I finally paid him twice what the ride was worth, even in hard currency rather than worthless rubles, he tossed the money on the seat and drove away in anger.

My wife recalls a similar financial farce she heard when she went to hear a talk by the editor of the *Moscow Guardian,* a paper that was launched a few years ago to reach the foreign community living in Moscow. Initially it was agreed that the paper would solicit customers who would pay for annual subscriptions. The Soviet editor suggested that a subscription price of $900 a year would be appropriate! The greatest irony of this story is a wonderful example of how a free market economy sometimes benefits the customer. So many firms were eager to reach the foreign community (one of the few market niches that had money) and pay $1,000 a page for advertisement space in the *Guardian* that the thirty-page weekly is now distributed free of charge.

Then there is my Russian colleague at Moscow State who asked me to collaborate with him on what was a truly excellent idea for a multivolume anthology of readings in Western Christianity. As general editor of the project he figured a salary to him of $2,000 a month for the duration of the three-year project would be adequate. We would also need to pay the editors and translators. Like my taxi driver friend, he had the greatest confidence that as an American I could arrange such a contract with a Western publisher. How could I explain that such an arrangement was virtually unheard of in America?!

Americans are not as rich as Soviet credulity imagines, nor is Western capitalism normally as greedy and criminal as some of the examples that now frequently occur in Moscow lead them to believe. American friends of ours here in Moscow rent an apartment from a middle man for $600 a month, who in turn keeps $580 and gives the remaining $20 to the owner. Not quite so bad but still disconcerting was our own experience. The middle man insisted on receiving $150 a month of the $650 apartment rent as a fee for finding our landlord a tenant. A friend hired a driver in St. Petersburg from a middle man for $15 a day; the middle man kept $10 and gave the driver, who worked up to sixteen hours a day for my friend, a paltry $5. Russians see examples of crooks like these and wrongly think this is what capitalism endorses. It is hard to explain that while capitalism does have its Michael Milkens and Ivan Boeskys, these people are convicted criminals, and that most Americans despise such greed. Unfortunately, what often happens is that Russian people see such ripoffs as typical of capitalism, and then reject the idea of a market economy as evil.[4]

Everyday Life: Difficult but Good

Early in our experience in Moscow I formulated a distinction in my mind that proved essential not merely to survive in Moscow but also to flourish. I concluded that life here is hard, but that it can also be good, even very good. Life in the former Soviet Union is arduous, and it can exact a price in terms of body, mind, and spirit. The weeks and months can grind you down. The harsh winters bring not only bitter cold but pitch darkness by 3:00 P.M. Urban summers in Moscow bring sweltering heat and aggravated pollution. But life here can also be very beautiful. The Western press often portrays the immense and complex difficulties here; and those difficulties should not be ignored if for no other reason than that most Westerners could deepen their level of empathy and increase their efforts to help. The fact is that many people, foreigners and native alike, do not like living in Moscow; disillusionment, apathy, stoic resignation, and negativism are widespread. But that is only half of the story, and it must be complemented by recognition of the rewards and joys of life here.

Difficulties

People in the foreign community especially, about 80,000 strong (estimates vary), find life here difficult. This is a telling fact because most businesspeople, correspondents, and diplomats receive hard-currency salaries, often supplemented with extra compensation for a

4. Cf. John-Thor Dahlburg, "Moscow's Neo-Capitalists Learning the Art of the Rip-Off," *NewsFax, Moscow Edition* (*Los Angeles Times*), March 2, 1992. Hereafter cited as *NF*.

"hardship" post (as with American Embassy employees). As a result they live at a much higher standard of living than they could in their home countries, and at an astronomically higher position than virtually any local resident. A recent poll of foreigners reveals widespread dissatisfaction with life and work in Moscow.[5] Only 10 percent of businesspeople came here for the money. Some 60 percent were sent here by their companies, while only 24 percent are here because they wanted to be. Seventy-four percent of them rate Moscow as "average" or "below average" in comparison with other places in which to work; 90 percent rate it as "average" or "below average" as a place in which to live. Expatriates here often feel exploited by a local economy that is ravenous for their hard currency and will do almost anything to extort it. (Imagine living in a country where many people and places of business refuse to accept your own, national currency.) Less than half stay longer than two years. Simple business needs become frustrating labryinths, like finding office space, establishing telecommunications, or obtaining normal banking services. In many ways the foreign community in Russia remains aloof from local life, deliberately insulated and isolated, perhaps for emotional protection. On numerous occasions Russian friends were incredulous that we would want to relocate here, and flabbergasted when they learned we brought three children. "Your wife is a hero!" our Russian friends have exclaimed on several occasions. I agree.

Lest anyone think that this is just another case of Western ethnocentricity, think again. Ride the metro and you see that many Soviets epitomize stoic resignation. Passengers either sleep, read a book, or, most commonly, stare mutely into space with blank expressions. Pass by a military-tough babushka wielding her pick-axe or snow shovel, or shoveling asphalt on a summer road crew, and you realize something has gone very wrong here. Watch with fascination as a clerk tallies your purchase with the ubiquitous abacus and you get an idea of how backwards life remains. Observe how people are forced to hoard the most basic of foodstuffs (one apartment I

5. The following figures are from an opinion poll that was taken by PBN Company, a U.S.-based public relations firm, and GLS Research, a San Francisco polling company, the first ever to survey Moscow's foreign community. See the *Moscow Guardian*, October 4, 1991, pp. 1, 3, 4.

visited had three refrigerators) and you understand their ominous projections about the future. Go to your local bread store and find it empty or even closed for days at a time and wonder how people who must live on rubles survive. On your way to work pass by the same food lines at the same stores week after week and marvel at how disastrous the Soviet distribution system is (and getting worse in Moscow because other republics grow the food and now resist sending it to the capital they have resented for so long). Witness two women vent their frustrations at waiting in line for four hours at the laundry mat by screaming and thrashing each other with their handbags, and you discover the depth of their pent-up anger. Walk through most public buildings that rarely have more than a third of their lights working and see a government that has become indifferent or unable to redress even the most basic of living conditions—a burned-out light bulb. Consider the average monthly salary of about $5 and rub your eyes in disbelief. Read figures about the brain drain and wonder where the next generation of leadership will come from. In a recent opinion poll released by the Soviet Center for Public Opinion and Market Research (VCIOM), the pessimism quotient runs high.[6] In short, for all but a very few individuals, life in Moscow is very difficult.

The breadth and depth of the problems facing the former Soviet society are truly overwhelming. Examples are legion. Living quarters are unimaginative, small, overcrowded, and spartan (most people live with three generations in two- or three-room apartments). In the apartments I stayed at in Sumgait, a suburb of Azerbaijan with a population of 400,000, we never had hot water, and at times we had no water at all. People who have apartments do almost anything to keep them in the family from generation to generation. People like my departmental colleague who do not have apartments in Moscow remain on waiting lists year after year and continue to commute several hours a day to work in Moscow. When I asked Sasha if he could help me to get a telephone in our dorm room, he quipped, "First, I dream about an apartment. Only after that can I dream about a telephone." He has been on a waiting list for three years.

6. See *The Moscow News* 52 (December 29, 1991–January 5, 1992), pp. 1, 6, 7. Hereafter cited as *MN*.

Crime is on the rise, with foreigners as common targets. According to interior ministry officials, about 7,500 crimes against foreigners were registered in Moscow during the period 1981–86, while in 1990 alone there were 7,674.[7] Auto vandalism is a special problem for foreigners because Moscow still requires all expatriates to have color- and number-coded license plates, making their vehicles easy targets. With a third of the former country's 300 airports closed, and those that remain open experiencing severe fuel shortages, air travel remains a dicey gamble. A friend of mine spent eighteen hours and had to make three trips to the airport before leaving on his flight from Moscow to the Ukraine; he was lucky to get there at all.[8] Health care remains primitive, even dangerous, not because of a poor scientific community but because of the lack of facilities and supplies. Ethnic strife and border disputes threaten to undo the fledgling Commonwealth of Independent States as the problems in Ukraine, Georgia, Moldavia, Tajikistan, Armenia, and Azerbaijan attest.

Joys

But apart from these many hardships that plague both foreigners and natives, life in the former Soviet Union can be immensely rich and rewarding. To omit this aspect of life here would be to leave my reader with a half-truth that fails to capture the irony and paradox of contemporary life in Russia. Russian hospitality is legendary, as we have experienced on numerous occasions. Julia, who lived above us with her boyfriend Slava and their two children in little more than fifty square feet in a single dorm room at Moscow State, insisted on having our family of five in their "home" for a full course dinner. How did the nine of us ever fit into that cubicle of a room?! Never for a moment was there any hint of embarrassment on their part, but rather the joy of sharing a delightful meal with us. They had even purchased champagne for the special occasion, something I knew was costly indeed. But Julia's hospitality has extended far beyond that delicious meal. She has showered us with an embarrassing number of gifts: a wonderful meat dish, a map of the

7. *MG,* November 11, 1991, pp. 1, 3.
8. For an interesting glimpse of travel within the Soviet Union, see Rod Nordland, "No Room at the Inns," *Newsweek,* December 2, 1991, pp. 71c–71i.

Moscow bus system, toys and candy for our children, magazines, tickets to the children's theater, spices for my wife, a guided tour of Moscow's children's library, and a Christmas bottle of vodka for yours truly! Julia is only one of many Muscovites whose hospitality has made life here for our family very good. Space does not permit me to relate similar warm memories about Victor, Cyril, and Lucia of Rostov-on-Don; Victor and Galena of Vilnius; Sergei Popov of Alma-Ata (Kazakhstan); or the family of Mamedov Nariman Allahverdi ogli of Azerbaijan who sent me home with fresh peach preserves and assorted nuts from the family dacha, a portrait of Mohammed, a bottle of Azeri cognac, and homemade bakklava.

Kindness rivals hospitality as a truly Russian trait that makes living here a joy. The delightful tradition of giving flowers, sold at almost any metro station the year round, symbolizes a deeper joy that difficult living conditions cannot suppress. Russian people tend to be kind to a fault, especially to vulnerable foreigners in need. On one occasion our family of five was at the metro station only to discover that we did not have the proper change for the ride. We went back outside to discuss the matter, and decided to make a small purchase in order to obtain the requisite change. But before I could find a kiosk, a man who had observed our dilemma tapped me on the shoulder and gave us the proper change, not only for our destination but for our return trip. I couldn't help but wonder if this would have happened to a foreigner at the New York or Chicago subway station. My wife will never forget standing in bitter cold weather at the long ruble-line at Pizza Hut with our children, and suddenly being ushered to the front of the line and afterwards helped by a total stranger who carried the take-home pizzas for her. On a different occasion my four-year-old son and I boarded a crowded bus and three different men instantly rose to offer us seats. It bothered me to recall an American journalist who just a few days earlier had told me that he could not give me and my son a ride home from a birthday party, or even to the metro a block away, because he was going in the opposite direction; we walked to the metro in the October rain.

My friend Hans, a language professor from Amsterdam who has taught on Moscow State's philological faculty on numerous occasions, helped me to crystalize another facet of Soviet life that we have enjoyed. One evening at dinner he remarked to me that "children here are sacred." After some reflection, I think he is right. Because economic depravity here is so severe and the apartments are so cramped, most families have only one child (and many abortions), and that child becomes a special object of delight and a symbol of hope for a better future. Several would-be emigres have remarked to me that they were leaving Moscow "for their children's sake." How many times has a babushka accosted my three children at the bus stop to yank on their hoods or lecture us that we must zip up their coats, put hats and scarves on them, or that in general they were just not dressed warmly enough? Sickness is a constant threat, and with primitive health care, one does not expose a child to anything that could cause an illness. Infants are a special delight to Russians and grant one the automatic privilege of cutting to the front of any of the ubiquitous long lines, an advantage our baby daughter, Megan, conferred on us any number of times (not the least of which was on our regular trips to McDonald's!). Children likewise assist one in hailing a cab, for who can resist stopping for a mother and father with three straggling kids standing in the bitter cold?! A wide variety of cultural opportunities in Moscow are directed specifically to children, including the famous Moscow Circus, Children's Musical Theater, the Central Children's Theater, the Moscow Puppet Theater, and Obraztsov Puppet Theater. Newspapers like the *Guardian* have separate sections that list cultural events designed for children. Children add special liabilities in Moscow, but they also signal another unusual joy about life here.

But Moscow offers an even richer brew of history and culture for adults. New Year's Eve 1991 our family dined at McDonald's and then hopped a bus down Gorky Street to Red Square, the literal and symbolic center not only of the city but the entire former country. People from across the world strolled around the large square that night in anticipation of the evening's events that would end with a midnight fireworks display. We stopped and tried to communicate with a group of university students from China who had admired our baby Megan. Television cameras with big satellite dishes were poised adjacent to the nineteenth-century Historical Museum. Powerful floodlights highlighted the heavy snow blowing in the frigid wind and bathed the surrounding buildings in a shower of light. St. Basil's Cathedral with its nine brightly colored and exotic domes, originally built by Ivan the Terrible from 1555 to 1561 to celebrate his defeat of the Mongol capital of Kazan, stood in stately splendor at one end of the square.[9] Photography vendors, taking capitalistic advantage of the breath-taking background and the changing calendar, solicited passers-by to pose for pictures (we obliged: 80 rubles). Lenin's somber mausoleum had attracted two screaming procommunist protesters, one holding a picture of the founder of the Soviet state, the other brandishing the now meaningless red and yellow Soviet flag. On one side, the GUM shopping mall was decorated for the holiday season; on the other, the yellow Senate Kremlin buildings behind the massive fortress walls flew the red, blue, and white flag of the Russian republic. The passing of the years from 1991 to 1992 heightened our sense of the passage of time and the movement of history in a great land. It also made us think about the rich, 1,000-year history of this people and its culture, and the role it has played in world history. In art, literature, music, theater, ballet, and architecture Moscow offers almost unlimited treasures. Where else could one go for such a richly rewarding experience? The hardships we had endured suddenly paled in significance.

At one point in my thinking, I used to ask myself whether the Soviet Union was anything more than an impoverished third world country with a large military. In some ways the analogy applies. Intractable social, political, and economic problems aggravate human suffering, and will continue to do so for decades to come. But in another sense the people of the former Soviet Union, their hospitality, kindness, attitude toward children, and long history of cultural riches, all explode the metaphor. Life in the Soviet Union is hard, but as paradox would have it, it can also be very good.

The West Looks East: Premature Optimism?

Another initial impression I have had regarding the former Soviet Union concerns the other side of the Atlantic and American per-

---

9. Legend has it that Ivan had the architects of St. Basil's, Barma and Postnik, blinded "in order that they could never produce anything better." Four years after Ivan's death (in 1588), however, they added to the church.

ceptions of my host country. Although I will address Russian politics
and religion in subsequent chapters, I would suggest that there exists
the possibility of American naivete about two very important matters
in Russia: the fall of communism and uncertain rise of market economics and democratic politics; and the depth and nature of spiritual
hunger here.

The Fortunes of Democratic Capitalism

First, Americans need to be cautious about overestimating the
current strength of and prospects for Russian democratic capitalism
and underestimating the possibility of a wholesale reaction against
political and economic reforms. Have we been a bit premature,
naive, and even triumphalistic in our euphoric optimism about the
fall of communism and birth of democracy? Of course we can rejoice
at the many wonderful changes that have taken place here, but the
future remains both complex and uncertain. Many difficult questions remain unanswered.

The Western press has televised the economic plight of Russian
people into our living rooms almost every night, but we must never
forget that these hardships constitute a compelling, empirical argu-
ment for many people that Gorbachev's initiation of reforms, and
even more so Yeltsin's radical economic plan that liberalized prices in
January 1992, have only led the nation into a twilight zone of economic disaster. One evening my wife and I enjoyed dinner at a
favorite Russian restaurant, one of the few places where the menu still
allowed one to pay in rubles. Although the price had doubled since
we had been there a few weeks earlier, our bill still totaled only $3.
When we returned to our dorm room we enjoyed a few minutes of
conversation with two women students from my class who had
babysat for us. I made the mistake of mentioning how delicious our
meal was, when I suddenly remembered how grueling life was for
them, especially the daily task of finding food. In her broken English
Natasha remarked, "Oh, going to a restaurant is not the normal
way for us. Things are very bad." Then, shaking her head from side
to side, she said something that has stuck in my mind: "Things were
better the old way." Many people in Russia find Natasha's logic very
convincing: What good is freedom of speech and press if you cannot

even buy a loaf of bread? You can't eat glasnost. The cure seems far worse than the disease. I was reminded of the African proverb that "an empty belly has no ears." How long will Russians continue to listen to reform-minded leaders when their shelves contain little more than bread, onions, and potatoes? Americans must understand that when Russians argue that "times were better" in the recent past they are not romanticizing the past or employing hyperbole; they mean those words literally, and in some instances they are right. Totalitarian socialism at least had the benefit of consumer prices that were both low and stable, and shelves that had a good selection of products—something early capitalism cannot yet claim.

Economic hardship poses a genuine threat to democratic reform and constitutes a powerful incentive for many to long for the ways of the past. Yeltsin promised that things would get better by the fall of 1992, but that was far too optimistic and little more than political rhetoric. Jeffrey Sachs of Harvard, the architect of economic reform in Poland and one of Yeltsin's economic gurus who urged the so-called shock therapy approach for the Russian economy, is not so optimistic. He has insisted that the economic conditions in Russia will get much worse before they get any better, and likened the reform to "jumping out of an airplane while you are still sewing the parachute. But they have no choice—the plane is crashing."[10] People who point to the examples of Poland and Hungary must remember that these countries had market economies before the war, a reality older people living there today remember and understand. Those conditions do not hold true in the former Soviet Union, where the ways and means of market economics are both strange and suspect. Further, the jury is still out on Poland, where in their 1991 elections the communists gained enough votes to force the formation of a coalition government. It is frightening to recall that the Bolshevik Revolution of 1917 followed Lenin's promise to feed the people. Let us hope history does not repeat itself.

But already ominous signs have appeared. Just two weeks after Gorbachev resigned on Christmas Day 1991, people in Yeltsin's

---

10. Quoted in *Time*, January 13, 1992, p. 26. In fact, Sachs has tried to shield Yeltsin from criticism by laying part of the blame for the nation's economic woes on the parliament and the central bank.

own Russian parliament, including the speaker of the parliament, Ruslin I. Khasbulatov, called for Yeltsin to dismiss his cabinet (and, by implication, for Yeltsin himself to resign). His own vice president, Alexander Rutskoi, has accused Yeltsin of "economic genocide." On Sunday, January 12, 1992, a procommunist rally of 5,000 people protested in Manezh Square (adjacent to Red Square and the Kremlin). One of the protesters, Marina Matkovskaya, a chemical engineer, put it this way: "These are bitter days for us. We see everything that our parents and grandparents built over seven decades being destroyed. We see our country being divided and its pieces auctioned off. We see a president [Yeltsin] who virtually seized power ruling by *ukaz* [decree] like a czar." The protesters' solution to the country's problems was a military takeover. They urged the military to "fulfill its constitutional duty and take authority into its own hands." According to Yegor Popovich, a Moscow city official, "The army is the guardian of the nation and the only protector we have left. . . . These so-called democrats seized power" and now they "are turning the whole country into a stinking whorehouse. They say that perestroika brought us out of the 'era of stagnation,' but no one starved in those days."[11] Popovich is wrong about starvation "in those days" (famines in Russia killed millions of people in 1921–22, 1932–33, and 1947–48), a protest of this size is not very large, and many people who passed by the crowds heckled them as fascists, but nevertheless it is a reminder of the deep hostility many people have toward economic reform.

Political and ethnic strife could also undo the fragile gains made by democracy. The examples of the Ukraine and Georgia demonstrate how uncertain the path toward reform is and how complex some of the questions truly are. The Ukraine, a nation roughly the size of France (50 million people), has insisted on ownership and control of both the conventional army on its soil (about 300,000 troops) and the prestigious Black Sea Fleet headquartered at Sevastopol. The fleet is important for both symbolic and strategic reasons. It has formed the nucleus of the Russian Imperial Navy since the eighteenth century, and its location connecting the Black Sea with the Mediter-

11. Michael Parks, *NF,* January 13, 1992.

ranean and then the Atlantic Ocean makes it strategic. According to a British research center, the International Institute for Strategic Studies, the fleet consists of 45 surface warships, 28 submarines, more than 300 other vessels, 151 combat aircraft, and 85 helicopters.[12] The Ukraine has also demanded that troops on its soil take an oath of allegiance. Yeltsin has declared just as vehemently that the fleet "was, is, and will be Russia's." In short, Russia has taken a posture that it is the primary inheritor of most of the former Soviet Union's assets, while the Ukraine is just the first of perhaps many republics demanding parity. Azerbaijan, Moldavia, and Armenia have likewise declared their intentions to have their own armies.

The example of Georgia is equally instructive and frightening. David Shipler, a former Moscow correspondent for the *New York Times,* comments on Georgia as an example of just how difficult it will be to establish democracy in the former republics. Zviad Gamsakhurdia has been a zealous Georgian nationalist and staunch anticommunist fighting for the republic's independence for nearly twenty years. In May 1991 he was elected president of the new nation in a landslide victory. Only months later, however, Gamsakhurdia proved himself to be little more than a dictator by silencing the press, jailing opponents, using violence against ethnic minorities, and refusing to share power with his parliament. Opposition forces then overthrew him in a violent coup that left 73 people dead and 400 wounded. Under seige for two weeks two floors underground in the basement of the parliament building, he finally fled Tbilisi in the darkness of early dawn for neighboring Armenia from where Georgians sought to extradite him. To the end Gamsakhurdia insisted the issue should be settled by a democratic referendum by the people, but it was not to be. A provisional emergency government (actually, a military council), took power, eliminated the post of the presidency, and indicated that parliamentary elections would be held in April. Meanwhile, Gamsakhurdia's supporters urged him to return to power. It was precisely these sorts of totalitarian lurches by the new "democratic" rulers like Yeltsin, Kravchuk of the Ukraine, Shushkevich of Minsk, and Gamsakhurdia that Gorbachev protested in his resignation speech.

---

12. *The International Herald Tribune,* January 9, 1992, pp. 1f. Hereafter cited as *IHT.*

Adding to the complex irony, another native Georgian, Eduard Shevardnadze, has now returned to his homeland to help rebuild a truly democratic government. The sad irony here is that prior to his genuine conversion to democratic principles, Shevardnadze was the oppressor in the 1970s, a hard-line communist who suppressed human rights in Georgia and imprisoned the dissident Gamsakhurdia. Shipler concludes, "the turnabout from the 1970s, when Mr. Shevardnadze was the oppressor and Mr. Gamsakhurdia the voice of liberty, humbles anyone who wants to believe in human predictability. . . . Elections alone obviously do not make democracy."[13] In late March 1992 the United States finally established diplomatic relations with Georgia, the last of the fifteen republics to receive formal diplomatic recognition from our country.

Do we really appreciate how fragile and uncertain democracy here is, Russia's historical propensity for autocracy, the social dislocation recent events have caused the average citizen, the depth of ethnic hostilities, the heated passions over border disputes (as between Armenia and Azerbaijan in Nagorno-Karabakh), and the powerful incentive all of these factors constitute for many Russians to despise reform? We must appreciate the enormous complexity of creating ex nihilo the mechanisms of an entire economic system, and the strange nature that political democracy holds for people here. Enormously complicated questions remain. Which former republics are responsible to pay back $70 to 80 billion of foreign debt accrued by a government that no longer exists? How should the army be parceled out to the 12 former republics—an army of 3.7 million troops, 10,000 combat aircraft, 56,000 tanks, 90,000 artillery pieces, and 800 warships? Who now owns all of the buildings, land, and cultural treasures of the former government? What is the relationship between the Russian Republic and Moscow's city government (Moscow's mayor, Gavril Popov, finally resigned due to disagreements with Gorbachev and Yeltsin). In our euphoria at the fall of communism and the fragile beginnings of political and economic reform, we must remember that the drama is still in its earliest stages.

13. David K. Shipler, "Democracy Needs Help in the Flip-Flop Republics," *IHT,* January 10, 1992, p. 6.

The last chapter has hardly been written; naivete and premature optimism by the West only aggravate the situation.

The Breadth and Depth of Spiritual Hunger

Americans might also do well to beware of their naivete regarding the religious situation in the former Soviet Union. Russia is neither as godless as some suppose (it has a 1,000-year history of Christianity, dating back to the baptism of Prince Vladimir I of Kiev in 988) nor as hungry for the gospel as presentations by some Western mission groups might claim. I would not question the spiritual needs of Russia or the presence of a genuine moral vacuum. Further, my experience has been limited primarily to university students, whose intellectual skepticism runs higher than that of the rest of the population. I would simply caution Western Christians that many here are not as openly eager to receive Christian envoys from America and their message as we might wish. By some accounts from Russian pastors, requests from the West "to help" have reached deluge proportions (one source documents 800 different Christian groups now working in Eastern Europe and the former Soviet Union; see Appendix C). Further, for those people who do seek to change, reorienting one's worldview is not a simple process.

In my own experience at Moscow State University, I have been surprised at the almost cavalier attitude of my students toward the Christian gospel. Only one or two of them would even consider themselves theists. A few of them entertain a radical historical skepticism that questions whether Jesus even existed. I would judge that our seminar in which we read *Mere Christianity* by C. S. Lewis (whom they did not know) had only a negligible impact on their thinking. Most of them tell me that they sense no existential need for religion. While they would resist the label "atheist" as a pejorative ideological remnant of the fallen Communist party, they would be quite comfortable in explaining to you that they were "nonreligious." Dig a little deeper and they would probably identify themselves as agnostics, believing that faith in God is fraught with insurmountable intellectual problems, a philosophical Gordian knot that no one can untie. They are unfailingly polite and kind, never hostile, but their interest in the subject matter is a professional or "scientific" one as they might say, not a practical or experiential one. Often what religious interest Russian people have is directed not so much to the gospel but to a hodge-podge of cults, occults, sects, astrology, and plain old religious hocus-pocus that can be found at most metro stations.

One day in our lectures on the basics of a Christian worldview, I finished explaining the doctrine of God, and then asked for my students' responses. A sampler of their comments is both instructive and revealing for those who are convinced of tremendous spiritual hunger in Russia:

Natasha: "We cannot laugh at Christianity; it has a 2,000-year history, and some of the best minds have believed in it. But I do not believe in God, and especially about the idea that people can have a personal relationship with him."

Svetlana: "I agree with only one thing you have said, that every person has a need for religion; but I cannot agree with you about the existence of God. I have no need to believe in God."

Vika: "The main obstacle to my belief in God is my education; I have no need for religion."

Lena: "I want to have faith, to believe in God, but for me it is impossible."

Vasily: "I want to believe in God, in real right and wrong, but I don't. But I don't want to believe right and wrong are merely relative either. God is closed to me."

Lena (from a different class): "I'm an atheist, and people sometimes feel sorry for me! They tell me, 'You'll get over it,' or 'Look! Just go to church—everyone is believing.' Today it is popular to show your religion. But for me it is too serious a matter to associate with these popular expressions of religion."

When I expressed amazement at their remarks, Natalia said I should not be surprised. She described herself as a "scientific materialist." Apparently unaware of the implicit dichotomy in her thinking, she indicated that her interest in our subject matter was scientific but not personal. In one sense Natalia was correct. From a practical standpoint it is naive of us Westerners to think that people who have committed themselves to a lifetime of atheist thought (professors), or have been educated for twenty years in a system where atheism was not only a basic presupposition but an obligatory ideology (students), would be able, even if they were willing, to change their entire worldview in a few short weeks or months based on a short religious presentation. One friend of mine, Ayo Ojajune, a Nigerian research scholar who has lived in Moscow some ten years, put it in perspective when he cautioned me to remember that "today's democratists were yesterday's atheists and communists."

I would even venture to say that far from witnessing the spiritual hunger of Russian people, I have observed that Marxist hostility toward religion has been very successful indeed at eliminating the felt need for God from many people. One rainy fall day in October 1991 I had the opportunity to visit a local public high school in Moscow and speak to fifty or more high school students and teachers about the meaning of Christianity. All of the students and teachers spoke impeccable English, so our communication process went well. In all honesty, based on the questions the students asked me, I felt like a Martian who had descended into a very friendly but foreign land. They were totally ignorant of the most basic religious issues and concepts. Afterwards I spoke to one of the teachers. She thanked me for my presentation and said it was very interesting. I asked her if she had any religious background or upbringing. No, she said. Sometimes she was interested in religion, but it was very hard to think about changing a lifetime of worldview commitments. As we drove home that day, it seemed to me that Marxist atheism had taken an eraser to the collective cultural memory of an entire people and wiped it clean. What remained was at best a tabula rasa, and at worst an ideological and truly unscientific prejudice against religion. Yes, they were very curious and full of questions, polite and receptive like few audiences in America. They presented me a large bouquet of flowers and urged me to return. But I sensed that their interest was more of an academic or cultural one, and only in rare instances a spiritual one.

One evening my younger son Andrew and I ate dinner together at Moscow State's student cafeteria. Exhibiting typical Russian kindness, a student and his girlfriend helped us to order our meals and urged us to sit down and eat with them. After a rambling conversation that included the girl's desire to visit America in order to see

Disneyland (I told them they could do that in Paris, something they did not know), I asked Svetlana if she was religious. No, she said. She had visited church once or twice, during the millennial celebration of Russian Christianity in 1988, but in general she did not have time for religion. I then asked her that since she did not believe in God, if she considered herself an atheist. "No, we don't believe in the atheists either. We don't believe in anything," she said.

Perhaps these brief remarks about American naivete regarding the reception of religion in Russia should be read as a minority report. I would guess the majority report about deep spiritual hunger in Russia contains some truth. I would never discourage missionary efforts here. Quite the opposite. I am part of one and would urge people and organizations to do all they can. If my analysis is correct we need more not less help in the former Soviet Union, but it needs to be the right kind of help. Efforts must be carried out with sobermindedness, cultural sensitivity, and a clear understanding about the past and present status of religion. We should opt for the long view with patience and perseverance rather than the quick fix that is sometimes more sizzle than steak.

A Prognosis for Perestroika: Reform or Reaction?

A fourth impression I have had about the former Soviet Union is that most people and institutions here are genuinely serious about wanting change and honestly seek to bring it about. Most of them endorse the idea of perestroika and are open to the so-called new-thinking. Gorbachev and Yeltsin provide an interesting contrast on this issue.

Gorbachev and Yeltsin

Russian people hated Gorbachev for economic reasons, not because they wanted to retain the Soviet system. In other words, many would insist that he could have brought about the good changes they all desired without the economic dislocation they have experienced, and they would have followed him if he had done so. Whether that was possible is doubtful, but it illustrates that people were open to change. They did not reject change; they rejected the economic price they were having to pay for it. Ironically, Gorbachev, the very person who instituted perestroika, never went far enough. He was never able to gauge the incredible desire for change indicated by signs like growing nationalisms that demanded self-determination (recall that he allowed troops to quash an uprising in Vilnius as late as January 1991), and intellectual dissent that insisted on human rights and free speech. He remained behind the curve rather than ahead of it, a committed socialist who wanted to reform rather than replace the communist system. In his book *The August Coup,* for example, Gorbachev wrote that he was convinced that the discrediting of socialism was a "passing fad." Months after he was deposed, in his first syndicated newspaper editorial he argued that "the idea of socialism lives on."[14] He simply could not reconcile himself and his thinking to historical realities. Ironically, Americans continue to credit Gorbachev with the full-fledged reform he tried to prevent.

Yeltsin, on the other hand, was able to read people's aspirations for radical change and to parlay them into being elected president of the repubic after having been sacked months before by Gorbachev. He has attempted to bring it about. He stood boldly for democracy during the coup plotted by cronies whom Gorbachev, the would-be reformer, had appointed; he has supported self-determination by the former republics; he has charted a course that totally rejects rather than repairs Soviet communism; and, unlike the many half-measures taken by Gorbachev, he has staked his very political life on the shock therapy treatment he ordered that began with the liberalization of prices January 2, 1992. In one sense Yeltsin and Gorbachev will share the same fate; they both will be vulnerable to the limits of people's patience and desire for change in the face of economic catastrophe. If radical reform fails, it will not be because people did not want change; it will be because the price was too high and the promises took too long to deliver.

Moscow State University

Another example of the genuine desire for change comes from my own experiences at Moscow State University. Several older departments that were bastions of Soviet ideology, like the Depart-

14. Mikhail Gorbachev, "Settled Down, Socialism Settles In," *NF,* February 25, 1992.

ment of Marxist Philosophy and Scientific Socialism, have been eliminated; others like my own have been renamed and now struggle to
survive. My own department has had four names in the past few
years. Originally the Department of "Scientific Atheism," it changed
to the Department of the "History and Theory of Religion and
Atheism." Later that was changed to "Religion and Freethinking,"
and in March 1992 it assumed the name "Philosophy of Religion
and Religious Studies." Although name changes come easy, true
reform of the department is incremental and slow, and ideological
differences sometimes divide younger and older scholars. But the
name change is more than cosmetic. I suspect the department must
justify its existence now that its ideological function has vanished.
Several of my Russian professor colleagues have spoken with approval
about the need for university education and society to be "depoliti-
cized" and "departyized." One of them even joked that perhaps
some day our department would be known as the Department of
Christianity. Of course he was not serious, but his remark was
another example of the powerful currents of change that now course
through Russia's finest university.

I was pleasantly surprised when one day a colleague asked me to
help redesign the departmental curriculum to make it more "uni-
versal," by which he meant they wanted to bring it up to Western
standards. They were delighted when I returned to Moscow from a
trip home and brought them some twenty sample curriculums of
philosophy of religion programs in American universities. They were
likewise thrilled to receive some 800 books on Christian studies that
our organization donated to the department. These books, the dean
and vice rector told me, would help them move beyond decades of
"parochialism" (their own word). While they still teach courses like
Marxist thought, for example, the requisite approach now is historical rather than ideological.

Threats to Perestroika

Threats to perestroika remain. Reform and restructuring could
well give way to reaction and a longing for the good old days of
economic stability. The cults of Lenin and Stalin are alive and well.
On a recent trip through Moscow's Sheremetyevo Airport I was

interested to see a rack of pro-Leninist literature in both English and Russian. A family visit to Lenin's mausoleum made a graphic impression on our family. Much debate continues in Moscow about whether to bury Lenin's body as the necessary final rejection of communism, or whether to leave it on display in the mausoleum in Red Square and continue to allow people to view it. Eager for my children to see Lenin's body before it was removed, we took the family to Red Square one weekend. Pro-Leninist rallies are not unusual in Red Square, but I was aghast to see that Stalin's tomb behind the mausoleum was buried in a mountain of fresh flowers strewn by devotees.

Many Soviets long for a powerful leader who will assume control, eliminate the chaos caused by perestroika, and restore stability to society. In one poll, more than 70 percent of the respondents indicated that they thought only a strong leader could guide Russia to prosperity. Older pensioners on fixed incomes who face the brunt of inflation are often the ones who long for a new Stalin. Maria Ivanova, a retired dishwasher, says she would "hang Gorbachev from a tree." As for Stalin, "I still love him!" According to Igor Tarasov, "The most important thing is that Stalin took care of the working class. Back then, we were drinking vodka and eating caviar. I make more money now, but I can't use it. Everything is more expensive." Mikhail Gerasimov argues that "this land needs a master who will keep the Russians in line. . . . Everyone talks about needing a new political leader who will take care of the country . . . I never had to think of food before now."[15]

Colleagues at the university illustrate this ambivalent state of affairs. Two professors in my department are in the vanguard of those who are catalyzing change and eager for any and all contacts with Western colleagues; but they also invited me to participate in a rally protesting the fallout of economic disintegration that they must face every day. In a personal conversation with Vladimir Dobrenkov, a former vice rector of the university who had jurisdiction over nine humanities faculties, he related to me the intense personal pressures he and the president faced as they tried to navigate the university through the push and pull of swift currents from both left- and

15. Jonathan Peterson, *NF,* October 1, 1991.

right-wing factions. In March 1992 the president of the university stepped down, and Dobrenkov left his administrative post to chair the sociology faculty. Perestroika is on everyone's agenda, but where it will lead or how far it will proceed remains to be seen.

Glasnost: Openness or Repression?

Glasnost or "openness" is one of the greatest legacies left by Gorbachev to a society that has been ruled by crushing repression, rigid censorship, and brutal control of every facet of civic life. As with perestroika, no one should doubt that glasnost is for real, but it likewise remains susceptible to disturbing relics of repression and passions of prejudice that remind us that past gains are no guarantee of future freedoms.

New Freedoms

I still marvel at how quickly freedom of speech and press has come to the former Soviet Union. Daily newspapers carry stories that just a few years ago would have doomed their authors to a lifetime of Siberian imprisonment. The long tradition of privately published dissent literature (*samizdat*) now finds publishers eager to print works that were written ten or twenty years ago and only now can be released to the public. Critical denunciations of Lenin and Stalin now appear frequently, as in the 1987 movie *Repentance,* widely shown even in the West. Social problems of drugs, sex, alcoholism, and pornography are openly admitted. Alexander Solzhnitsyn has indicated he will return to his homeland after completing his current writing projects. Dissident Andrei Sakharov was finally released before he died. Religious freedom now exists in ways it hasn't for 100 years. As I indicated before, in my teaching at the university I have never encountered any restrictions of any kind. I was given a literal carte blanche to say and do what I pleased.

Old Repressions

But the legacy of repression still exists in ways both large and small, real and imagined. Habituated for seventy years in a mode of fear, many people still harbor deep suspicion, paranoia, and distrust.

Victor remains convinced his phone is still tapped. Vasily assures me that mine is, too. Andrei is concerned that real estate agents are really mafia thugs. Lena refuses to come to my dorm room at Moscow State University because of her memories of the security guards that even today still spot check identification cards of those attempting to pass through the gates. Mikhail, a psychologist friend, literally stopped in his tracks, his face blanched, when he saw the uniformed Russian guards at the home of the American ambassador (Spasso House) where we had taken him for a Christmas Eve communion service. When foreigners register their vehicles they are still issued license plates coded by color, numbers, and letters (for example, red plates indicate diplomats, "K" identifies a correspondent, and the prefix 004 would refer to an American). Two groups of people in particular, long the targets of hatred in many countries, also illustrate the problems of lingering repression that would threaten glasnost: Jews and homosexuals.

I personally hold to a traditional Christian view of homosexuality, that it is a sin, but I likewise support civil rights for all people. On this issue, at least, the Christian is challenged to protect and promote civil rights while at the same time discouraging moral wrongs. Censorship and censureship are two different things.

In a country that for seventy years has considered state rights to be far more important than individual rights, Article 121 from Stalin's penal code still considers homosexuality a crime punishable by up to five years in prison. In fact, as recently as October 1991 a person living near Sverdlovsk was jailed for allegedly infecting another man with AIDS, even though no formal complaint was filed. Soviet officials were so indignant when the first HIV case was diagnosed in 1985 that they charged that the infection was a case of American "germ warfare." Overt and explicit discussions of AIDS prevention is still considered pornographic. The World Health Organization has sharply criticized Russia's policy on AIDS testing and prevention. In 1987 Soviet government figures showed no recorded cases of AIDS, and current figures are still considered "ridiculously low."[16] Consequently, and we might say for both good and for ill,

---

16. *Moscow Times*, March 24, 1992, p. 4. Hereafter cited as *MT*. Cf. also *MT*, March 27, 1992.

the gay movement in the Soviet Union lags far behind its Western counterparts. More recently, however, gays have linked their cause to the democratic movement and policy of glasnost that, theoretically, should insure civil rights to all citizens. About 100 gay activists are vocal in Moscow and in the last few years new gay periodicals have appeared (*Tema, Ty, Risk,* and *Argo*), along with the "Russian Union of Gays and Lesbians." Moscow's first gay conference was held in the summer of 1991. Co-sponsored by the International Gay and Lesbian Human Rights Commission (San Francisco), the week-long conference passed without incident and featured films and speakers. Only a year earlier a riot almost broke out at a rally where participants distributed free condoms.

For most Russians, however, homosexuality is perceived as an illness to be tolerated, and harassment follows those who have "come out of the closet." According to Igor Cohn of the USSR Academy of Science, who has studied the nation's sexual attitudes for over fifteen years, "gays are still the most hated social group in the country." In a 1990 poll by the Union Center of Public Opinion and Trade Research, 33 percent of respondents said gays should be "liquidated," 6 percent indicated they should be helped, and 30 percent said they should be left alone. Because of hostilities like these, gays are especially vulnerable to AIDS. While there is an AIDS hotline, the government has offered no help at all to these people who are still considered criminals and consequently imprisoned.[17]

The Jewish community in Russia also has good reasons to doubt the guarantees of glasnost. On one of my several trips to St. Petersburg I stumbled upon a fierce anti-Semitic rally in Palace Square, behind the Hermitage Museum. Signs demanded that "Jews go home!" Protests still continue over the Lenin Library's refusal to honor a court order to hand over 12,000 Jewish holy books of the Schneerson Collection, which was confiscated in 1917 and sealed in the library archives. Anti-Semitic literature and hate groups like the Pamyat Society demonstrate with flags that bear the Nazi swastika. Jewish emigration from the former Soviet Union has increased in recent years (184,268 Soviets emigrated to Israel in 1990, and 106,000 in the first eight months of 1991), but many Soviet Jews

17. See "Coming Out of the Closet," *MG*, December 5, 1991, pp. 1, 4, 7.

face the undesirable option of returning from Israel due to unemployment (as high as 40 percent for immigrants) and culture shock. More than half of those arriving in Israel warn friends back in the Soviet Union not to come. The alternative of staying in the Soviet Union, though, is likewise unappealing to many Jews. One poll indicated 39 percent of Jews in the Soviet Union feared pogroms. Another poll by the Confederation of Jewish Organizations and Communities (Vaad) revealed even more ominous trends in two-thirds of the formerly Soviet population: 5 to 7 percent of the former Soviet Union's non-Jewish population considered themselves dedicated anti-Semites; 20 percent considered themselves "traditional" anti-Semites; and 40 percent indicated that their attitudes toward Jews were generally negative.[18]

As with perestroika, the gains made by glasnost are tangible but also ambivalent and even uncertain. Consolidating the recent gains will require considerable vigilance on the part of all of us who desire genuine restructuring and true openness in the former Soviet Union.

Conclusion: An Uncertain Future

Everyone wants to know where recent events in the former Soviet Union will lead. Because I have lived in the country for a while, people often ask me this question. I wish I knew the answer. The most truthful response—even if it is not very satisfying—is that no one knows. The fifteen former republics of the former Soviet Union, now each a sovereign nation, sail uncharted waters. Ask a Muscovite what he thinks about it all and he is likely to shrug his shoulders and throw up his hands. One issue, however, is at the top of everyone's list: economic survival.

18. See "Back to the USSR," *Newsweek*, November 18, 1991, p. 21; Yakov Borovoi, "The Jewish Dilemma," *New Times* (Moscow) 41 (1991): 23.

3

The Eclipse
of the Abacus:
Economics

This is the fourth gasoline station I've stopped at, and no
one has any gasoline. I waited 40 minutes at the last station, and then they ran out. I'm fed up with this kind of
life!

—Sergei Fyodorov
Refrigerator technician

I keep hoping that one day all this idiocy will stop. First
they raise the price on gasoline—which is bad enough—
but then they run out. It's long past time for the state to
give up its monopoly on gasoline.

—Yuri
Russian Foreign
Ministry[1]

1. Elizabeth Shogren, *NF*, April 21, 1992.

Introduction

Disinterest in Politics

When you talk to many Russian people, from a Western perspective it comes as somewhat of a surprise to learn of their general disinterest in politics. Russian sociologist and pollster Yuri Levada has suggested that Russians are simply a "nation tired of politics."[2] Resignation and apathy remain the order of the day. Speak to a cabbie about Gorbachev, winner of the Nobel Peace Prize and *Time* magazine's "Man of the Decade" (1980s), or Yeltsin, the populist champion of democracy who slayed the dragon of communism, and the response is rarely more than a shrug of the shoulders and a turn of the hands upward. On certain days you might receive a wave of the hand, or a mad slash at the air, as if to dismiss the issue altogether. Nor do you hear much discussion about how the former Soviet Union should destroy or redistribute its 27,000 nuclear warheads, what should be done about the dispute with the Ukraine over the prestigious Black Sea Fleet, the formation of new nationalist armies, new religious freedoms, fuel shortages, airport closings, or ethnic strife in the former republics—all those thorny issues that exercise Western analysts.

Priority of Economics

One concern preempts all others and remains at the top of every Russian's list, as President Yeltsin found out on his domestic trips to promote his reform policies: economics. At every stop Yeltsin was heckled when he tried to explain the need for economic transformation. Prices had skyrocketed and shelves remained empty. In Moscow, for example, sugar and milk remain scarce, a kilo of cheese costs a week's wages, gasoline prices quintupled overnight, and consumers are angry. When I speak to professors, administrators, and students at Moscow State, they make it clear that the economic crisis has made serious scholarship and concentrated study today difficult at best and for most simply impossible. Endless hours in food

2. Interview with Yuri Levada, *Newsweek,* April 6, 1992, p. 58.

lines or moonlighting three to four jobs to put food on the table makes serious intellectual inquiry a luxury that few can afford, to say nothing of the mental and emotional energy required to maintain even this subsistence lifestyle. Several professors have told me that publishers do not have any paper to publish their work. From the pensioner to the professor, from the babushka to the scientist, economic issues overshadow all others. The country's economic problems, and what to do about them, are truly complex, of course, but from the economic perspective of the average person in the street, the matter is simple: You cannot eat glasnost.

The Crises of Economics

If the economy is an urgent priority for most people, the movement from a centralized command structure to a supply-demand market system is also a convoluted, baffling, and even mysterious process for them (including the experts). Why shouldn't it be? Moreover, no one, not even in Eastern Europe, has ever successfully managed to transform a command economy into a market economy. In economics, as in other spheres of its life and culture, Russia is a melange of glaring contrasts, radical upheaval, and breath-taking backwardness. Two examples stand out in my experience.

How can it be that in the technologically advanced country that shocked the world by launching the first artificial satellite on October 4, 1957 (*Sputnik*), in many places an old babushka still calculates your purchase with lightning speed on an abacus. An abacus?! Yes, loud clicking sounds rather than the familiar blips and bleeps of the computer scanner greet shoppers in many places of commerce, for the abacus is ubiquitous here. It symbolizes the economic lethargy of the past and the startling complexity that the nation faces in retooling its economy for the age of global commerce. While the European Community moves toward a single monetary currency by the end of the decade, Russia languishes in the economic outback, struggling to replace the abacus with the computer. By the way, for the forseeable future, the computers that must replace the abacus will have to be imported, for no one in their right mind would purchase a computer built in Russia (say, the ES 1841 made in Minsk or the Neiron made in Kiev). Most people in the know consider these computers "unreliable," to put it politely. Vnesheconombank (the Federal Bank for Foreign Economic Affairs), "the very symbol of the Soviet economy in the outside world," did not purchase its first computer until the 1970s and today not a single one of its computers was built in the former Soviet Union. In Russian computer circles an aphorism explains the matter: "A Soviet computer is entirely compatible with itself."[3]

How can it be that in Moscow, a city of 10 million people and an 800-year history of commerce, arguably the second most important city in the world, until very recently there was only one, tiny little place—the American Express "office"—in the entire city where a person could obtain hard currency? I use quotation marks, for the office is really little more than several large cubicles. People with only Visa or Mastercard are out of luck. Forget the automatic teller, too; it limits customers to withdrawals of 250 rubles (about $2). Recently I needed $2,500 in U.S. dollars, so I headed down to the American Express office. Although I should consider myself fortunate that the transaction was even possible (what do expatriates in Kiev do?!), completing the process takes unusual patience, for one must negotiate two different lines to receive only travelers checks, and then take those checks across town to another bank that will cash them (if they haven't run out of hard currency). It used to be a little simpler; until this fall you could cash the travelers checks next door at Vnesheconombank, but Vnesheconombank is now bankrupt.[4] Still, who am I to complain? Even economic heavyweights like CNN and Monsanto have been prevented from withdrawing money from their own Vnesheconombank hard-currency accounts.[5]

Thus, economic matters loom large for nearly all Muscovites, and for most of them the current upheaval is a strange, foreboding, and hostile territory. The twin perils of the devaluation of the ruble and inflation of consumer prices illustrate just how catastrophic the eco-

3. Cited in "Computing the Country," *Moscow Magazine,* December 1991–January 1992, pp. 69–77. In 1987 the country had about 150,000 personal computers, the United States about 25 million. Today the United States has about 60 million PCs, the Former Soviet Union 300,000.

4. Yegor Gaidar, Russia's economic minister, declared the bank officially bankrupt in mid-December 1991.

5. *MG,* December 6, 1991, pp. 1, 3.

nomic problems in Russia are. The issue of hunger and the availability of food shows how foggy the situation can be. The nascent beginnings of capitalism and the possibility of aid from the West exemplify possible ways to eclipse the age of the abacus and move into the economic twenty-first century before it is too late.

The Ruble as Rubble: A Deflated Currency

A Mountain of Money

Autumn was upon us and it was time to buy twenty to thirty Christmas gifts for friends and family I could take home with me on my brief trip back to the United States at Thanksgiving time. This required some extra rubles and after weeks of procrastination I finally headed down to the American Express office at 21a Sadovo Kudrinskaya on the ring road. After waiting in the two different lines and receiving my hard currency (Vnesheconombank was not yet bankrupt at that time), I asked to change some of my U.S. dollars into rubles. The clerk obliged, and when I gave her $300 she returned from the bank vault with several stacks of bills, each about six inches high. I felt like I needed a backpack to haul the little mountain of money home. It was a graphic lesson that no economic textbook or lecture could ever teach me about the meaning of a currency that had lost almost all value.

The World of the Ruble

Russians sometimes refer to their currency as the "wooden ruble." In a recent issue of a news magazine one writer commented that the ruble has now entered the realm of funny money. His point is well taken, that today the ruble is almost worthless (literally and not just figuratively speaking), but the economic gravity of the deflation of the ruble's value is anything but funny. Imagine living in a country where the largest bill minted is worth about $40 (a 5,000 ruble note, which, incidentally, is the first Russian note without Lenin's picture on it); where some stores and restaurants will not allow you to pay for your purchase with your nation's currency; where to buy an airplane ticket you have to obtain currency from a different nation;

where an overnight train ride from Moscow to Nizhni Novgorod (Gorky) costs 60 cents, a gallon of gas about 5 cents, a loaf of bread 2 cents, and a ride on Moscow's famed subway system one tenth of a penny (15 kopecks). Welcome to the world of the ruble!

Five Ruble Rates

One problem with the ruble has been the government's past practice, finally but only gradually being discontinued now, of drastically overvaluing the ruble.[6] In fact, the "value" of the ruble varies drastically depending on which of five different rates one uses to calculate its worth. Until it was discontinued early in 1992, the old commercial rate had been set by the government at about 1.7 rubles to the dollar (thus 1 ruble was equal to about 60 cents). This rate was required of all transactions by foreign governments and firms, both Soviet and foreign, that earned hard currency. In fact, the primary purpose of this outrageous overvaluation was very simple: It allowed the Russian government to extract hard currency from businesses and governments living here, which in turn helped the Russian government service its foreign debt and buy badly needed imports for the state.

In January 1992 this old commercial rate was discontinued and replaced with a new commercial rate, which was set at 55 rubles to a dollar, a vast improvement over the 1.7 figure but still a gross overvaluation. The tourist exchange rate set by the central bank of Russia now stands at 110 rubles to a dollar, and various exchange points offer the tourist anywhere from 90 to 117. That rate makes the ruble equal to about a penny, although some bankers anticipate that this rate will increase to as high as 200 rubles a dollar, making the ruble worth half a penny. Theoretically, the rise of this tourist rate toward market realities should make the black market rate obsolete, for the difference in the two rates should become negligible and thus there would be no incentive to trade dollars for rubles on the sly. But as I write, the black market rate will fetch 140 rubles a dollar, 30 percent higher than the official tourist exchange rate. On the inter-

6. Unless otherwise noted, all figures that follow apply to the rates effective in late January 1992. As of November 1992 the ruble had plummeted to 400 to the dollar.

national commodities markets, large Soviet enterprises with healthy balance sheets sell the ruble at the auction rate, which now stands at about 150 to 180 rubles to the dollar—presumably the ruble's "real" worth for those who need to buy them in large quantities. Contrast the shocking disparity between the old commercial rate (1 ruble worth about 60 cents) and the international auction rate (1 ruble worth less than a penny), and you get an idea of the convoluted state of economic affairs in the former Soviet Union.

Ruble Free Fall

While the government has tried to prop up the value of the ruble, even it has had to recognize reality and make concessions to the decreasing value of the currency. Simply put, in the last six months of 1991 the value of the ruble nose-dived in a free fall, with no clear end in sight. Just a year or so ago the ruble was worth about $2. When we moved to Moscow in September 1991, the official tourist exchange rate was 32 rubles to the dollar, which made the ruble worth 3 cents. On November 4, 1991, the government raised the rate to 47 rubles to the dollar, and in December 1991 to 110 rubles a dollar. Comparing the official tourist rate of 32 of September 1991 to the black market rate of 140 in February 1992 demonstrates that the rate has nearly quintupled in five months.

Related Aggravations

Several other interrelated matters have aggravated the devaluation of the ruble. The government's response to the problem of inflation—to print more and more rubles—is a classic recipe for hyperinflation (too much money chasing too few goods). In the Brezhnev era, for example, the State Administration for the Issue of Banknotes (Goznak) issued to the public about a billion rubles a *year*; today, it is printing 18 billion rubles a *month*. For the first time ever, in late 1991, 200 and 500 ruble notes were printed (500 rubles equaled a month's salary then); 5,000 ruble notes appeared in the summer of 1992. In fairness, the central bank would respond that printing more rubles is almost the only way they can pay the army and meet its payroll. When the government allowed stores to open in Moscow that operated with only hard currency (restaurants, grocery stores, department stores), it forced the helpless ruble to compete with the dollar, and drove its value down even faster. Dollar stores in Moscow also created discrimination against cities in other provinces that did not have them and which, consequently, cannot obtain goods and services that only the dollar can purchase. Most of the former republics have declared they intend to introduce their own national currencies (Azerbaijan, Estonia, Lithuania, Latvia, Moldavia, Kazakhstan, Georgia, and Ukraine). The process is easier said than done, and no country has followed through yet, but the Ukraine has already printed a new currency (the grivna).[7] Early on both the Ukraine and Byelorussia introduced "money" in the form of coupons that could be used more than once and that were necessary to purchase some basic food and consumer goods. In the spring of 1992, just after Russia was admitted to the International Monetary Fund, its government announced it would make the ruble fully convertible by August 1992, set at a value of 80 rubles to the dollar and bolstered by the IMF's stabilization fund. But since this convertible rate was set by the government and not by the free market, many Western businesspeople in Moscow greeted the news with skepticism.

Examples of the Consequences

Practically speaking, what all this means is that the dollar has de facto replaced the ruble as the standard currency in major cities of the former Soviet Union (less so in small towns and villages), so that people and institutions in Russia will do almost anything to avoid receiving rubles and conversely try to do anything to obtain hard currency. Many examples come to mind. Westerners renting apartments in Moscow must pay from $400 to $2,000 a month or more in hard currency, depending on the location, for normal Russian apartments that by Western standards are spartan. It is not unusual for landlords to request three months' advanced rent so that they can purchase airfare or pay for medical care. One Western executive commented to me that his corporation paid $6,000 a month

---

7. Facts and figures in this paragraph were taken from *MN*, November 10–17, 1991.

for his 1,200 square foot apartment; another apartment I was in cost the tenant's government $4,500 a month.

Foreign students studying in Russian universities and institutes used to receive monthly stipends along with free tuition, but now in many instances those stipends have been revoked and international students are charged tuition that must be paid in hard currency. Such a reversal in economic policies earned the Pushkin Institute in Moscow $1 million in 1990, according to its vice director of international relations. The effect of such policies, of course, has been to reduce drastically the number of foreign students enrolled in the former Soviet Union. Cuba sent some 4,200 students to the former Soviet Union in 1990, but only half that many in 1991. Eight hundred Vietnamese studied in Moscow a few years ago, but only 300 in 1992.[8]

I will never forget the response of one old, wizened cabbie when I told him I would pay him only in rubles. He reached into the front pocket of his dirty old jacket and pulled out a wad of rubles that would have choked a horse. In mock anger he snarled, spat on the rubles, and jerked his hand as if to toss them out the window. When I asked the owner of an apartment what he would do with the dollars in rental money I offered to pay him each month, a veritable king's ransom by Russian standards, he tried to explain to me that it was really not that much, because many items of normal life (a car or home repair, for example) could be had only by paying dollars. Airlines now require Russians to pay for tickets in ruble prices that equal dollar values, making travel to other countries a virtual impossibility for most people. On more than one occasion I have had Russian students knock at our dorm room wanting to trade rubles for our dollars in order to enable them to purchase a plane ticket to Europe. Then there was the vendor at a flea market who just laughed at me when I tried to purchase my souvenir in rubles rather than the hard currency he demanded. "The ruble isn't money," he exclaimed. "It's only paper!" The sad part about the displacement of the ruble by the dollar is that most Russians do not have dollars, do not have access to dollars, and, consequently, are sometimes not

8. Figures cited in this paragraph are from *MG*, November 1, 1991, pp. 1, 3.

able to obtain even simple services like a taxi ride, because the drivers refuse to accept anything but hard currency. One Russian friend who had just been rebuffed by a cabbie turned to me and said, "You see, Dan, our money does not work!" Thus, it is easy to empathize with their anger at being required to purchase goods they cannot afford in a currency they do not have.

Sticker Shock at the Kiosks: Inflated Prices

Introduction

Theoretically, if a ride on the Moscow subway costs only a fraction of a penny, and bread only a penny or two a loaf, then Muscovites should be able to survive well enough on the average monthly income of 500 rubles (about $4). But in this instance theory and practice are two different things. While the value of the ruble has plummeted, consumer prices have sykrocketed, and in most instances wages have lagged far behind. And, as we shall see, even if wages were doubled or tripled, which is most unlikely, it would hardly be enough to keep up with the fires of hyperinflation now raging through the Russian economy. Furthermore, to date far too little privatization of the economy has occurred to stimulate competition and lower prices. In December 1991 alone, a month before Yeltsin removed most price controls on retail products, the inflation rate was at about 50 percent for the month.[9] Another analyst pegged inflation for the year 1991 at 450 percent.[10] The Associated Press reported, for example, that while the inflation rate for the first six months of 1992 was 787 percent, wages had increased only 103 percent. The many commercial kiosks or *komissionis* that line the sidewalks of most of Moscow's major thoroughfares, especially prevalent around subway stations, provide us with a paradigm of Russia's new free market and a street-level reflection of the inflationary woes that plague consumers.

9. Figure cited by *Time*, January 13, 1992, p. 26.
10. Cited in *The Wall Street Journal–Europe*, January 10, 1992, p. 6. Hereafter cited as *WSJE*.

The Kiosk as Paradigm

The Moscow kiosk is actually a micro-department store, barely large enough for one or two vendors to fit inside, which sells a potpourri of consumer goods at market prices for a commission, from candy bars and liquor, cosmetics and lingerie, to clothing and electronic gadgets. An official license is required to operate a kiosk, but virtually no controls exist over how vendors buy and sell their products. Prices have always been higher at these stores than at state-run stores where prices have been controlled by the government, but then again products are available at the kiosks that cannot be found at state stores. In some instances kiosk owners purchase goods from wholesalers in dollars and pass on the cost to the consumer. In recent months prices at the kiosks have exploded, due to scarcity of goods and panic buying. A winter coat, for example, can easily cost 4,000 rubles, and sometimes is hard to find at all. While such prices provide a windfall for the kiosks, it has been a nightmare for consumers.[11]

The Political Context

The political context of Russia's economic woes reveals a certain irony about the complex interplay between the vagaries of the populace and the conflicting loyalties forced on them by the benefits of new freedoms of speech and thought (glasnost) and the disadvantages brought on by the demise of communism and uncertain beginnings of a free market (perestroika). Gorbachev, the architect of both reform and restructuring, could never bring himself to do what the people never wanted anyway—completely abandon price controls. In effect, he dismantled many features of the communist command economy without replacing it. To the day of his resignation he recommended a "mixed economy" that combined state ownership and free market, what he called "a multitier economy" with "an equality of all forms of ownership." His inability to fulfill the promises of perestroika led to his rather ungraceful ouster by Yeltsin. Thus, Gorbachev never made a decisive move to a free market, a move that now that it is underway has provoked the ire of nearly all the Russian citizens.

11. See "Kiosks Steal the Show," *MG*, November 8, 1991, pp. 1, 17.

Yeltsin, on the other hand, dared to do what Gorbachev wouldn't and what people feared most. On January 2, 1991, just as he had been promising for months, he administered the so-called shock therapy to Russia's economy that liberalized prices by removing most controls that had kept consumer prices ridiculously low for decades. In July 1991, a month before the ill-fated August coup, Yeltsin rode a wave of democratic popularity all the way to the Russian White House presidency. Whether he can withstand the storm of consumer hostility remains to be seen. He no longer has Gorbachev to blame or to function as a lightning rod for criticisms; now he faces the brunt of voter wrath alone.

Only two weeks after the January 2 reforms were instituted, Yeltsin had to deflect criticisms by blaming state suppliers for deliberately sabotaging his reform program by producing high-cost luxury items rather than staple goods. One of his foreign economic advisers, Jeffrey Sachs of Harvard, likewise found others to blame, namely, the republic's central bank (for printing too much money) and parliament (for their failure to raise taxes and pare down the budget). Both groups have publically disapproved of Yeltsin's program. Ruslin I. Khasbulatov, speaker of the Russian parliament, has called for Yeltsin to fire his cabinet, and Georgi Matyukhin, chairman of the central bank, has complained that the "shock therapy" has only resulted in higher prices, empty shelves, and dangerous social unrest. Thus, Yeltsin faces his biggest challenge yet: to convince consumers that the chaos precipitated by radical market economic reform will eventually produce economic benefits similar to the freedoms of democracy brought about by glasnost. But the patience of many is wearing thin.

Consumer Responses

Responses to the January 2, 1992 price increases were delayed for a few days; some shops remained closed for the holidays, many consumers had hoarded products in a wave of panic buying, and some managers of state stores simply did not understand what was happening. But within days consumer wrath reached a crescendo. Pensioners, elderly people on fixed incomes, were hit hardest.[12]

12. Gorbachev's pension, for example, is a mere 4,000 rubles. Normal pensioners receive about 300 to 400 rubles a month.

Upon entering a store and seeing the new prices, one pensioner, Leonid, fumed: "What I've seen today is a major-league goddamn mess. The time will come to take a machine gun. . . . For now it's calm, it's the first day. But we veterans say there will be blood spilled in Moscow, and the women will start it because they have to feed their families."[13] Another pensioner, stunned by a sign advertising "premium" sausage for 500 rubles a kilo, described the situation as "a nightmare come true. . . . How can we live? My pension is only 350 rubles a month." Her wrath then focused on Yeltsin, whom she viewed with the same disdain as she did Gorbachev: "We have driven out one skunk, but another one is left."[14] Not all the critics are pensioners, either. Sergei Abramov, a twenty-seven-year-old school teacher, looked at a pound of ham that would have cost his entire month's salary. He then complained about the disparity between the blessings of free speech and the curses of free prices: "We trusted Yeltsin when he was fighting for democracy. But this is no longer a democracy—this is robbery of the people. If he doesn't change this his days are numbered."[15] The first week of February 1992, only a month after the price liberalizations, Moscow vice mayor Yuri Luzhkov said that the economic reforms had pushed 95 percent of Moscow's citizens below the poverty level.

Table of Prices

Exactly how bad is bad? The table in this section charts some of the price increases that consumers in Moscow faced after the January 2, 1992 price increases. In reading the chart, several factors must be kept in mind: First, 100 kopecks equal 1 ruble. Second, 1 kilogram equals 2.2 pounds. Third, although some make more and others less, the average Russian salary is about 500 rubles; in some instances, both the husband and wife work. Fourth, the following figures reflect prices immediately before and after the January 2, 1992 increases, but for a more accurate comparison one must remember that prices spiraled upwards long before and after January 2 (espe-

---

13. Carey Goldberg, *NF*, January 3, 1992.
14. *MG*, January 10, 1992, p. 1.
15. Goldberg, *NF*.

cially with the first major price increase in April 1991). For example, just *before* the January 1992 increase, a loaf of bread cost about 50 kopecks; after January 2 more than 2 rubles; but six months before the new year price hikes bread cost only 20 kopecks, and as I write today (August 1992) it costs 12 rubles. Thus, in this example, the price increase for bread is not merely fourfold (50 kopecks to 2 rubles) but sixtyfold (20 kopecks to 12 rubles). Fifth, some goods might be purchased for different prices at different types of stores (state store, kiosk, black market, open market). Prices at the markets are much higher, but the selections and quality may be better; prices at state shops are lower, but quality and quantity of products tend to be worse. Sixth, prices cited are accurate, but they are intended only as general examples that depend on various factors, for example, whether one purchases white or black bread, premium or normal grade sausage, and so on. Seventh, some basic foodstuffs like sugar, milk, cheese, and eggs are still scarce at state shops no matter what the price, or can be obtained only by standing in line for hours. Other products require a ration coupon (*vizitka*) which entitles the holder to a limited purchase per month (although having a coupon does not guarantee that the consumer will find the given item on store shelves). In compiling this chart I encountered an interesting phenomenon. When I asked Russian friends how much some of the basic foodstuffs like sugar, milk, and cheese cost, to a person they all responded that it had been so long since they either saw such a product or actually bought it that they couldn't remember the price. Eighth, sometimes consumers will barter one item (some homemade mayonnaise) for another (potatoes). Until local authorities stopped it by searching cars, some budding capitalists would travel 250 miles from Moscow to buy goods in outlying villages where prices were much lower and resell them back in the city at hiked up prices. Finally, keys to abbreviations are as follows: r=ruble, k=kopeck, pl=per liter, and pk=per kilo. By adding up the costs of a simple trip to the "grocery store," it does not take a mathematician to see that the Russian consumer faces a no-win situation. Truly, it is hard to know how they survive. Nor does this chart include other normal expenditures, like a man's suit that could cost 5,000 rubles.

Shock Therapy: The Price of Progress
Sample Prices Before and After
January 2, 1992 Liberalization

Item	Before	After	Aprox.% Change
Loaf of bread	50k	2-3r	400%
Milk (pl)	70k	3-5r	500%
Cheese (pk)	80r	400r	500%
eggs (10)	2.60r	12r	460%
Sugar (pk)	2.20r	7-10r	400%
Sour cream (pk)	26r	86r	330%
Butter (pk)	132r	240r	80%
Potatoes (pk)	15r	50r	333%
Tomatoes (pk)	60r	150r	150%
Sausage (pk)	30-40r	200-300r	700%
Macaroni (pk)	1r	10r	1000%
One Christmas cookie	30k	2.88r	950%
Bottle of beer	1.55r	8r	500%
Bottle of vodka	10r	45r	450%
Pack of cigarettes	25r	100r	400%
Gasoline (pl)	44k	1.20r	280%
Hair salon cut	45r	115r	250%
Copy of *Pravda*	30k	80k	270%
Chicken (pk)	7r	35r	500%
Big Mac	3.75r	60r	1500%

Is Russia Hungry?

The Fat Babushka

With their wages frozen, the buying power of their rubles plummeting, and their food costs skyrocketing, are Russian people hungry? How can they possibly survive when a kilo of cheese or sausage, providing one can even find them, costs a month's wages, and a pair of woman's winter boots at the kiosk costs two months' salary? What in the world do they eat? Night after night Western television news-

casts broadcast pictures from the former Soviet Union of crowds of
shoppers pushing and shoving or standing mutely in line, and store
clerks presiding over cavernous, barren state-run grocery stores. As
I began to contemplate this question during our early months in
Moscow, another perplexing question occurred to me. If the food
crisis here is so bad, why are so many babushkas so fat? Why do we
not find children with distended stomachs and skeletal rib-cages as we
all have seen from the recent famines in Somalia and Ethiopia? Are
Russians hungry? The answer to this question is both yes and no,
and it illustrates the complex economic problems that Russia now
faces.

Starvation and Hunger

We can safely say that very few people in Russia starve, and not
many even go hungry. Epidemic hunger as it exists in famine-stricken
Africa is unknown here. Unlike Africa, in terms of natural resources
the former Soviet Union is one of the richest nations on earth. Bad
weather has not hampered grain production this past year (although
1991's harvest was down about 25 percent from 1990's). According
to Alexei Yemelyanov, chair of Agricultural Economics at Moscow
State University, grain harvests for 1991 were about average (about
200 million tons for the last five years).[16] Per capita meat consumption in the former Soviet Union stands at about 134 pounds a year,
compared with 176 pounds a year for America.[17] But to leave the
matter at that would give a very misleading impression. Avoiding
hunger is one thing; a subsistence diet is another.

Meager Subsistence

The diets of most Soviets tend to be poorly balanced; babushkas
are fat because their primary staples are bread and potatoes. Most
Russian meat is of such poor quality (lots of fat and gristle) that
most Westerners would never buy it, much less eat it. Fresh fruits
and vegetables as the West knows them are either nonexistent or

16. Yuri Kotler, "The Farm Report," *Moscow Magazine,* October–November 1991, p.
68.
17. Carroll Bogert, "How Much Hunger?" *Newsweek,* December 2, 1991, p. 33.

very expensive (save carrots, onions, beets, and cabbage). Variety of foods is limited. Some bread shortages have occurred, for example, not because there was no bread, but because people bought more and more of it as a substitute for other food items not available and because of intermittent panic buying. For example, in the fall of 1991 the bread store at our university was barren for several days, and then it finally closed for a few more days. A common explanation was that the city had a normal supply of bread but that panic buying by hoarders created the shortages. Others suggested that antireform officials created the bread shortages as a form of political sabotage. More common still, sometimes stores will have only cheaper quality brown bread and not the better quality white bread. Thus, bread is almost always available, although it might take unusual persistence and endurance to obtain it. Steady diets of borscht, bread, potatoes, and cabbage prevent starvation, and can even make people overweight, but not much more than that.

Reasons for Shortages

Starvation is not a problem here, but chronic shortages are. Problems with the nation's food production are not caused by poor harvests, but by related aggravations like lack of fuel and spare parts for farm machinery; poor storage, transportation, and distribution systems (some estimates say 20 to 40 percent of the grain harvest never reaches consumers); collective farms that withhold meat and grain in hopes of higher prices in the future; graft that siphons off the better products before they ever reach the markets in order to sell them later at inflated prices or to enjoy them personally; poor work habits and the lack of a work ethic ("we pretend to work and they pretend to pay us," goes the Soviet workers' proverb), and so on. Bread, the all-important staple of every Russian diet, provides a good example of why chronic shortages persist. Grain and flour reserves are sufficient to produce enough bread for the city of Moscow. Shortages occur not because of insufficient supplies, but because of how the bread is made and distributed. Retailers order less bread than they can sell because of penalties they incur for every loaf they return, and stale bread, considered inedible according to social custom, is often returned to bakeries to be ground and used as filler in meats. An insufficient number of trucks prevents timely deliveries. For example, in one day some 2,300 tons of freshly baked bread were distributed to Moscow stores but that evening about 300 tons of it (13 percent) was returned as too old to eat.[18] All of these factors combined create the anomaly that, as Hedrick Smith has observed, Russia has an economic system where "massive waste and enormous shortages exist side by side."[19]

How They Do It

Even when hunger and shortages are averted, Russians pay a high price for their subsistence diet. Creativity, ingenuity, and luck combine forces to get most families through. If one cannot afford the expensive open markets, standing in long queues for hours to buy whatever the state shops might happen to have becomes a necessity. Ration coupons are required for some basic foodstuffs and limit customers to small monthly allotments. Buying, selling, and trading these coupons is itself a business. Many Russian citizens almost always carry a bag with them, called an *avoska* (literally, "maybe"), for you never know when you might stumble on an unexpected purchase; besides, in Russia you do not shop with a "grocery list," but for whatever is available. Many resort to dishonesty. When I asked one student how her mother survived, she responded, "It's impossible to live honestly on an average salary here." Many families live with three generations in a single apartment; supporting one another is a given. Bartering a tape recorder for a pair of shoes can solve the problem of insufficient rubles. At the open markets sellers line both sides of the sidewalk, holding out a single item to sell or trade—a pack of cigarettes, a kitten, a jar of honey, a kitchen faucet, a lone fish (stiff as a board!), slippers, a Barbie doll, literally almost anything to raise a few rubles or obtain a needed item. Knowing delivery schedules is a bonus. Some families make their clothes; buying them is out of the question. Hoarding is a common phenomenon. One

18. Louis Uchitelle, "Russia Is Long on Bread (and Longer on Lines)," *IHT,* January 23, 1992, pp. 1, 4.
19. Hedrick Smith, *The New Russians* (New York: Random House, 1990), p. 240.

apartment I visited had three refrigerators; another had a cupboard stuffed with a massive amount of food. In Bakarevo on the Volga River, near Yaroslavl, one family had a stash of fifteen sacks of potatoes, two barrels of salted cabbage, heaps of onions and carrots, five huge jars of pickles, and forty quarts of fruit preserves in their damp, earth cellar.[20] Such hoarding is not a sign of affluence but an indicator of people's economic pessimism about the future and near total distrust that the government's reform policies will make their lives any better. If one is especially fortunate, a plot in the countryside will yield some summer produce that can be canned and stored for the winter.

Yuri and Olga

Yuri (26) and Olga (24), a young couple from Moscow, and their daughter Katya (1), illustrate how an average Russian family avoids hunger by patching together a meager subsistence.[21] Their family lives in a "communal apartment" (*kommunalka*) that houses twenty people in ten rooms. They have little chance of obtaining a private apartment. Yuri is a medical assistant and works in a Moscow hospital emergency room; at night he moonlights at a privately owned newspaper. His after-tax income is about 900 rubles a month, a sum that only a year ago he considered a dream: "We weren't rich, and we couldn't save, but I could buy my daughter fruit at the market for 10 rubles a kilo instead of waiting in line to get it at 4 and not have to think about it." Olga is a medical student with a monthly student stipend of 150 rubles a month (she will earn 270 rubles a month when she graduates as a doctor). Thus, together they bring home about 1,000 rubles a month, nearly twice what many others make. But the challenge to subsist is great.

For food they rely on a combination of their personal stash; lucky finds at the market (as when Yuri happened on a fresh delivery of eggs; at 10 eggs for 12 rubles, he bought 40 eggs; another day he waited in line "only 40 minutes" to buy chicken steaks for 19 rubles a kilo); and their family and friends. "We are lucky," says Yuri, "in

20. John Kohan, "Unmerry Christmas," *Time*, December 30, 1991, p. 26.
21. The following story is taken from the *MG*, November–December 1991, pp. 1, 3.

that we have a large family. My brother and sister-in-law, my mother, my sister—we all help each other." Olga's mother retired early in order to take care of Katya each day from 8 A.M. to 4 P.M. while Olga attends medical school. "When I come home," says Olga, " I give her money and she goes and stands in line." For basics like potatoes, onions, and carrots, they shop at the state stores, but if they want fruit they must shop at the expensive open markets. If the market does not have an item, they do without. "I stopped drinking milk a long time ago," Yuri remarks.

Clothing is another matter. "We don't buy clothes," Olga remarks, "I sew everything." Their coats are five years old, and Yuri jokes that "if the moths eat my coat, I'm in trouble." Recently he was able to barter with a friend for a pair of Yugoslavian shoes. Clothes for Katya come almost exclusively as donations from friends and relatives. According to Olga, "It's the only way we can get them for her. . . . There is nothing in the state stores. It's frightening." For Olga's birthday Yuri bought her a "cheap 25 ruble dress," but that was fine with her. "If he bought me something expensive, I'd give it back so that I could buy some tomatoes. What good are expensive gifts if you don't have anything left over for the necessities?" For Yuri's birthday Olga knitted him a sweater.

How did their country arrive at this sad state of affairs? Although his answer is simplistic, it is also revealing. Citing corruption as the chief culprit, Yuri says, "People lived for seventy years in a system in which the only way to get by was to cheat. It's hard to expect that they'll become honest and hard-working just because they can." As an example he cited the large number of consumer goods that never reach the state store shelves but instead end up at commercial kiosks at greatly inflated prices.

Yuri, Olga, and Katya do not starve, nor do they go hungry, but in the Russian economy right now that is little cause for rejoicing. Motivated by "pride in being honest" and love for Katya, they eke out a sparse subsistence. Perhaps the greatest tragedy of all is in their outlook on life. Yuri has little hope for the future. "I really can't see anything that gives me the slightest reason to believe things will get any better soon."

On Capitalists and Yuppies: Self-Help

Capitalism Pro and Con

Is Russia's economic future hopeless? How can Russia, a land so rich and yet so poor, escape an economic meltdown caused by a battered currency, rampant inflation, and lifestyles of meager subsistence that escape hunger only by stealth and persistence? To simplify matters we can say that the nation must simultaneously pursue two courses of action: It must help itself, and it must receive help from its friends. In this section we will look at the nascent beginnings of capitalism as one (and only one) example of the first response, and in the following section the matter of international aid.

Many people in Russia hate "capitalists" and resent anyone who tries to get ahead of others. For many Russians—and no doubt this results from seven decades of socialist ideology that abolished all forms of private ownership and means of economic production— words like "capitalism," "immorality," and "decadence" are almost synonymous. Capitalists have traditionally been branded as *zhuliki,* scoundrels, even criminals, and to be a "Russian entrepreneur" was oxymoronic. The target of Yuri's scorn was clear when he referred to "businessmen interested in making quick money, not in building something lasting." Of course, some people would deserve Yuri's opprobrium: "real estate agents" who extort money from their clients, or middle men who do almost nothing to earn a fair wage for fair work. Capitalism, in America and Russia, can play on the greed of both buyer and seller. The ethical standards of capitalism in the former Soviet Union are especially problematic because of legal, municipal, and regulatory confusion. But hardly all Russian "capitalists" are cheats, nor do all Russians look on budding entrepreneurs with contempt. From the ten-year-old boys who scurry out into the traffic to clean windshields at stoplights, to people like my friends Alexei and his wife Irena who started their own computer software firm out of their apartment, Russians are learning the benefits of self-help. Times have changed, and with it the Russian vocabulary; *biznesmeni* are cropping up all over.

As might be expected, the new wave of Russian capitalists are primarily younger people who have not imbibed past ideology for as many years as their elders and who refuse to accept the deprivations their parents suffered. They reject communist socialism with a vengeance, demand a better way of life, and intend to work to make that a reality. In one opinion poll conducted by the Moscow Public Opinion Center, over half of the eighteen-to-thirty-five-year-olds responded that they perceive "the ability to conduct business" as a way to transcend the current economic morass. Leonid Seydov, a researcher from the research center who took this poll, observes that "Russians younger than 30 are keen on earning money and hard currency. They are business-minded."[22] Konstantin, a taxi driver, incarnates this new entrepreneurial zeal, albeit in a somewhat dubious fashion. He never stops to pick up Russians, and by catering only to hard-currency paying foreigners, he claims to make $400 a month working only fifteen days. "I want dollars, my friend, only dollars."[23]

Lena and Genia

One evening I was pleased to visit my friend Lena Spirkina, a thirty-five-year-old psychologist who, in the do-it-yourself spirit of self-help, has started a Christian graduate school of psychology in Moscow. Lena has incorporated her school, the Academic School of Professional Psychology, in both the United States (through friends at Fuller Seminary in California) and Russia, and it now operates out of the Russian Academy of Science's Institute of Psychology where Lena works. When I sat down at her kitchen table that chilly autumn evening in 1991 and she served me hot coffee brewed from a drip coffee-maker, a rare luxury seldom found even in nicer Moscow restaurants, I knew I had met a different type of Russian. Both she and her husband Peter earned their Ph.D.s at Moscow State University and both speak excellent English. Their apartment on Leninski Prospekt is considered a very desirable address in the city because of the better quality of the older apartment buildings— brick construction, tall ceilings, courtyards with trees, proximity to

---

22. Joanne Levine, "The Yuppies Are Coming," *MG*, November 8, 1991, p. 4.
23. Joanne Levine, "Taxi Drivers Adapt to New Fares," *MG*, January 24, 1992, p. 19.

the university and its intellectual community. They own their own car. Legos and a color television occupied their son when I visited them. When we went into Lena's home office, amidst her sea of books and stacks of papers befitting a scholar, I noticed a fax machine she uses to communicate with business friends she has made on her several trips to the United States. When I commented to Lena about all of these amenities, she startled me, saying quite seriously, "You see, Dan, we are yuppies." I laughed out loud, thought about it some more, and then determined that Lena was exactly right. The description fit.

I decided to teach at Lena's school in the Institute of Psychology (I still do), although I refused to accept her offer of payment. Instead, I decided to test this yuppie's networking skills. For our first ten weeks in Moscow my wife Patty washed all of our clothes by hand (for a family of five) because we could not find any househelp to employ. We had also failed to employ a driver. In a week or so Lena had secured both a girl to wash our clothes and a driver to take our son to school, dependable and extremely helpful people whose services we still appreciate today. Lena is only one of many examples of a younger generation pursuing the path of economic self-determination through hard work that eschews the ways of the socialist handout.

Genia, a twenty-six-year-old freelance translator, turns away work for hard currency because she is so busy. "Business comes to me," she once remarked to me. In early 1992 I called Genia to help me with my travel plans to the Baltics, but she apologized, and asked if she could be "direct" with me; she was booked for the next month and was not able to assist me. A graduate of Moscow Linguistic University, Genia speaks impeccable English and French. Her business card includes not only her home phone number but numbers for her fax and telex. When I asked, Genia gave me the pros and cons about a number of hard-currency restaurants in Moscow at which she had eaten. For Christmas 1991 she spent two weeks in France, only one of several such trips that has enabled her to purchase her stylish clothes. Genia works long hours (too long in my opinion), and like Lena, she is an exemplar of the new "do-what-it-takes" vanguard of Muscovite businesspeople.

Further Examples

I could multiply examples. College dropout Herman Sterligov, an economic wunderkind, claims to make 2 million rubles a day in profits from his Alisa, a trading company that he started a year ago. The frenetic energy of his employees and technological capacity of his offices, both atypical for most business establishments in Moscow, make one think he just might be telling the truth. "I like to make money," says Sterligov, age twenty-five, "and money makes more money." No wonder that he founded the Russian Millionaires Club, and that he intends to "topple what's left of Soviet power. . . . I'm doing everything by my work to make it happen more quickly." In downtown Moscow a Swedish joint-venture disco, Nightflight, attracts Russian yuppies who shell out $10 for the entrance fee and $5 for drinks.[24] *Moscow Magazine* recently devoted an entire issue to the top fifty businesspeople in the former Soviet Union, including people like world-renowned eye surgeon Stanislav Fyodorov, the magazine's "Businessman of the Year" (1991), who finances his hospital from a hard-currency casino he started, invests in a hard-currency hotel, set up a cellular phone network, purchased two collective farms in order to stock his hospitals with food, and trains his own Arabian horses he enjoys riding as a hobby; or Irina Razumnova, founder of Guildia, Moscow's first small business administration for women that assists would-be entrepreneurs through offering two-week training seminars for 800 rubles and one-on-one personal consultations.[25]

Persistent Problems

Despite success stories like these, legions of problems plague Russia's experiment with capitalism. Taxes provide an excellent example. I was shocked to learn from a Russian friend who had just started his own firm that the government taxes his profits at a rate of 45 percent (in addition to other taxes for revenues and so forth). His bank loans, initially secured at a 20 percent interest rate, increased to 50

24. Joanne Levine, "Yuppies Are Coming."
25. The last two examples are taken from *Moscow Magazine*, December 1991–January 1992, pp. 7, 50.

percent and then 80 percent. Russia's government has announced plans to institute a 28 percent "value-added tax" on all consumer goods. More incredible still, a law is now in effect that requires all foreigners living in Russia to pay a 60 percent income tax on their worldwide income. People who for decades have been paid almost nothing for doing almost nothing, and who in some instances have been forced to cheat in order to survive, find it difficult to appreciate the economic importance of reliability, honesty, efficiency, and customer service. Calculating the costs of overhead, raw materials, transportation, wages, inventory, research and development, and so forth are all very strange notions to most Russians, and well they should be; for the past seven decades they have been forced to accept unilateral decision making for literally everything from the government. Economic initiative was penalized, not rewarded. Many Muscovites still prefer the certainty of a meager but regular check from a centrally planned socialist government and the "stability" that comes with central control to the uncertain fortunes of capitalism's voyage into uncharted waters. One student of mine referred to this mindset as a society-wide kindergarten mentality. Western firms locating in Moscow must scale a mountain of logistical and ethical hurdles: a bankrupt Vnesheconombank whose replacement is not yet clear; laws that are constantly changing, murky, and often unknown by anyone; contracts that used to be negotiated by a single federal bureaucrat that are now in the hands of unknowns from fifteen nations; and a future that is anything but certain. "There's total chaos. Nobody knows who's responsible for what," laments Czechoslovakian businessman Igor Junas of Kerametal Foreign Trade Company.[26] I will never forget one Sunday in our English-language Protestant church when a Western businessman worshiping with our congregation for the first time stood up to introduce himself and announced that he had relocated in Moscow to work for a Western firm on a telecommunications project; the entire congregation of about 200 people erupted in spontaneous laughter. Privatization

---

26. Tim Carrington, "Western Firms Find Soviet Breakup Good—and Bad—for Them," *WSJE*, January 23, 1992, pp. 1–2. Firms now in the former Soviet Union include Westinghouse Electric, Polaroid, Reynolds Aluminum, Chevron, Digital Equipment, Gilette, Kodak, and AT&T.

still proceeds at a glacial pace; one figure indicated only thirty-eight shops in Moscow had been privatized.[27] In Russia alone half of the 2,300 joint-ventures have failed and are no longer open.[28] Suspicion of the federal and municipal governments persists. Even a plan of free privatization of apartments by Moscow's city government was greeted with skepticism by Muscovites who waited to see how much the taxes, unannounced when the plan was unveiled, would cost them. After seven decades of "mandated equality" some sectors of the economy that are faced with the freedom to set their own prices, like producers of bread, margarine, milk, eggs, and sausage, find price fixing rather than price competition a way to insure mutual survival. Moscow's thirty-one bread producers, for example, all buy their equipment and raw materials from a single consortium under which they are organized, the Moscow Bread Supply, which also keeps their financial books. The result, of course, is simply another form of monopolism, this time imposed by the consortiums instead of the government.[29]

Will Russia's experiment with capitalism work and move the country forward to self-sufficiency, productivity, and a maximization of its rich human and natural resources? Can capitalism survive the perils of a dangerously deflated currency and hyperinflated prices? Or will consumer fury, producer lethargy, and the near total lack of any market economy infrastructure cause it to backfire and lurch toward the old ways of central planning? No one knows, of course. It is far too early to make a determination. One thing, however, is certain. Russia cannot accomplish the task alone. If economic reform is to succeed, aid from the West to enable Russia to help itself will be necessary.

International Aid: Help from the West

Introduction

Since Gorbachev began to woo the West, the question of international aid to the former Soviet Union has exercised the minds of

27. Joanne Levine, "Getting By," *MG,* January 24, 1992, p. 3.
28. *WSJE,* January 24–25, 1992, p. 1.
29. Laura Hayes and Adi Ignatius, "Moscow's 'Capitalists' Decide the Best Price Is a Fixed One," *WSJE,* January 22, 1992, pp. 1, 2.

analysts. Although all able nations, especially those of Western Europe, Asia, and the oil-rich Persian Gulf, should insure Russia's successful reform through aggressive aid, for practical reasons I will focus on the role of the United States. A few people have discouraged such aid. During the 1992 presidential campaign Patrick Buchanan campaigned on the protectionistic and isolationistic slogan of "America First" and a platform that anathematized foreign aid. David Brooks, deputy editor of the *Wall Street Journal Europe*'s editorial page, has warned about fostering Russian dependence on outside help, a curious piece of logic given the magnitude of the country's problems.[30] A. Craig Copetas warns that "Russia is about to take America to the cleaners" and that assisting "Yeltsin's charismatic anarchy" will result in money down the drain.[31] I reject such thinking as morally flimsy, politically naive, and economically short-sighted. For a host of reasons, any number of which alone would be compelling, the West must help Russia.

Russia's proven resolve

During the Gorbachev years Western nations had reasons—good ones, too—to withhold aggressive aid to the former Soviet Union. Gorbachev intended to preserve rather than jettison socialism; he wanted to reform rather than replace communism. As late as January 1991, he sent troops into Lithuania to try to prevent the independence movement there. He opposed genuine self-determination and independence, as evidenced by his efforts to keep the Baltics in the USSR right up to the August coup and to maintain the former country through his planned "Union Treaty."

Under Yeltsin, however, the course of the country (now fifteen countries) is far different. As promised, with his January 2, 1992 liberalization of prices, Yeltsin has burned the bridges of communism behind him. In fact, with success not at all certain, Yeltsin has already risked his very political life on moving toward a form of democratic capitalism. Russia was not invited to the fifty-nation international aid conference held in Washington in late January 1992, but Yeltsin wrote a letter that was read to the delegates. In

---

30. David Brooks, "The Grand Temptation of Yegor Gaidar," *WSJE*, January 23, 1992, p. 6.
    31. A. Craig Copetas, "Help for Russians Would Be Money down the Drain," *IHT*, November 25, 1991, p. 4.

that letter he appealed for help by reminding conferees that Russia had "opted irrevocably for creating a civilized state" where individual needs were not subservient to the state, and he vowed he would create "the necessary legal guarantees for investment, economic activity and repatriation of profits." In an effort to calm fears about aid not reaching its final destination because of governmental corruption and confusion, he vowed that Russia would "take all measures that are necessary to ensure its delivery to concrete addresses and to ensure its fair distribution." The financial costs of the required help were astronomical, admitted Yeltsin, but, speaking with unusual candor, he reminded delegates that Russia had to "pay dearly for past mistakes and delusions." Yeltsin's first deputy prime minister, Gennadi Burbulis, has likewise reminded the West that "the program of radical reform undertaken by Russia is irreversible."[32] Whether the attempts at reform succeed or fall prey to right-wing conservatives who still exist in Russia's bureaucracy remains to be seen, but the clear intentions of Yeltsin, unlike Gorbachev, are to move fast forward to a democratic, free market society. That proven resolve deserves our support.

There is no better alternative

Writing in *Time* magazine, and again in his nationally televised speech on March 11, 1992, former President Richard Nixon, who did not favor extensive aid to the Gorbachev government but now favors helping Yeltsin, argues that Yeltsin has done an admirable job of assembling the best economic minds available in Russia. David Brooks refers to them as "fearsomely respected economists" and cites with approval Polish economist Jan Winiecki's judgment that they comprise "the best team that it is possible to collect in Russia."[33] Several expatriates are assisting their efforts, including Stanislav Gomulka and Jacek Rostowski of Poland, Richard Layard from the London School of Economics, Anders Aslund of Sweden, and Jeffrey Sachs of Harvard. Yeltsin himself has led an all-out effort, stumping around the country's small towns to urge people to have patience, and for now he has as much political capital as anyone to

32. Gennadi Burbulis, "Help Russia to Reform," *IHT*, January 23, 1992, p. 6.
33. Brooks, "Grand Temptation."

sell the program. According to Nixon, Yeltsin's group of economists is Russia's "A-team," but given Russia's shortage of qualified economists who understand what must be done, there is no "B-team." Writes Nixon, "If Yeltsin's reforms fail, no successor will be able to do any better."[34] Helping Russia now is the best opportunity the West has today or will have in the future.

The magnitude of the crisis

The crisis Russia now faces is not merely to survive a harsh winter or two; nor is the crisis merely one of food. The crisis the country now faces is truly catastrophic and will threaten her for decades to come at almost every level of society—politics, religion, economy, technology, medicine, culture, national defense, international relations, consumer production and consumption, environmental protection, and even the national psyche of its citizens. One woman, holding back tears, expressed the blow to her self-esteem in this way: "You cannot even conceive of the humiliation I feel. We are a great country. What has happened to us?"[35]

According to one estimate Russia will need some $30 billion a year for the next five years. Burbulis has asked for a "minimum amount" of $20 billion for a ruble stabilization fund, and for balance of payments support to enable crucial imports of food, medicine, subsidies, and credits, not to mention the deferral of 1992 interest payments on debt. Such figures far exceed the amounts of international aid now proposed by other nations. In the first quarter of 1992 alone Burbulis reported that Russia had to import ten tons of grain because of increasing bread consumption created by shortages of other foods.

Murray Feshbach, a demographer at Georgetown University who specializes in Russia, measures the gravity of the crisis in other ways, and expresses concern that the West has not yet understood the urgency of Russia's peril and how such ignorance exacerbates the crisis. According to Feshbach, some 1.5 million people will die in Russia this year because the country's health-care system lacks basic facilities and supplies. The food distribution system contaminates

---

34. Richard Nixon, "The Time Has Come to Help," *Time,* January 13, 1992, p. 27.
35. Kevin Klose, "Russians Think the Americans Could Help," *IHT,* November 26, 1991.

almost half of the baby food sold to consumers. Pollution causes one health ministry official to exclaim, "To live longer, breathe less." Life expectancy for Soviets has droppped. According to Feshbach, "The spread of malnutrition will lead to disease, in a country that has no aspirin, let alone more sophisticated medicines. The spread of disease will lead to lower production and much less efficiency . . . in a country that has 50 Chernobyl-type atomic reactors in operation (one of which near St. Petersburg leaked in April 1992)."[36]

In light of the magnitude of Russia's crisis, the responses from the international community have been too slow and too meager. Nixon warns that the American response has been "pathetically inadequate." Burbulis puts the matter in perspective by noting that from December 1990 through December 1991, $1.4 billion of humanitarian aid reached the former Soviet Union—250,000 tons from 60 countries— but this only amounted to the equivalent of one day's worth of nationwide consumption. By early 1992 the United States had pledged total aid to Russia worth $4.6 billion, but the vast majority of this (over 80 percent) was in the form of credits to allow Russia to purchase American grain. U.S. aid for food and medicine totaled just $300 million. Germany, in contrast, has pledged a total of $37 billion. The largest portion of that commitment ($13 billion) will go toward removing and housing the 370,000 Soviet troops that were in East Germany. About $735 million of Germany's aid is designated for food and medicine. During the aid conference held in Washington in January 1992, Bonn complained that it had anted up 70 to 90 percent of all the aid given to the new Commonwealth of Independent States; in 1991 alone Germany's help totaled $18 billion. One-third of the former Soviet Union's $70 billion foreign debt is owed to Germany. Thus, they were right to urge other nations, especially Japan and the Persian Gulf states, to bear their share of the burden. The magnitude of Russia's crisis demands it.

The high cost of failure

It does not take much imagination to fathom how costly the failure of successful reform could be. If for no other reason than selfish regard or enlightened self-interest to sidestep a looming catastro-

---

36. Jim Hoagland, "Government's Responses to the Crisis Have Been Feeble So Far," *IHT,* January 23, 1992, p. 6.

phe, the United States can avoid paying later by paying now. Russia still has an unsecured military, including 27,000 nuclear warheads. Libya has tried to employ Russian nuclear scientists, while Kazakhstan officials have admitted that on December 20, 1991, an SS-19 intercontinental ballistic missile launch occurred without their knowledge. Food riots have occurred among university students in Tashkent, the capital of Uzbekistan. When more than 1,000 students protested the January 16, 1991 price increases there, the military forcibly dispersed them with sub-machine guns and truncheons. At least one student was killed. In Tbilisi, Georgia, the nation teeters on the brink of civil war between supporters of the deposed (but democratically elected) totalitarian nationalist Zviad Gamsakhurdia, those who ousted him in a coup, and recently returned Georgian native Eduard Shevardnaze. In Estonia Prime Minister Edgar Savisaar resigned on January 23, 1991, barely a year after the republic gained independence. Russian's historical propensity for autocracy and authoritarian leaders is not lost on the U.S. Ambassador to Moscow, Robert Strauss: "I'd rather risk a couple of billion bucks out here for our country than fail to risk a couple of billion bucks and end up looking at a real fascist-type situation."[37] If Yeltsin fails and is replaced by hard-liners, the international community will find itself in another crisis "that would make the meagerness of its current aid program seem penny-wise and pound-foolish."[38] Nixon has expressed the same sentiment: "To put it bluntly, Russian President Boris Yeltsin and those like him in other republics must not fail."[39] The cost of such a failure would be far too great, far greater than the aid presently needed to insure success.

A cold war quid pro quo

Many observers have rightly drawn attention to the opportunity the West and its allies now have to parlay the military savings resulting from the end of the cold war into constructive aid to help the former Soviet Union. By all accounts the current military threat of the former Soviet Union is gone. Troops and officers are greatly

37. Leslie Gelb, "Failing to Help Russia Would Shame America," *IHT*, November 25, 1991, p. 4.
38. Strobe Talbott, "A State That Deserved to Die," *Time*, December 30, 1991, p. 28.
39 Nixon, "Time Has Come."

disillusioned at their fallen status, uncertain salaries, declining living standards, and chaotic order of command that remains to be sorted out among the fifteen former republics (at this writing, for example, Soviet troops were still stationed in the Baltics because Yeltsin's government simply has no money to bring them home and house them). The country's projected military procurements for the first quarter of 1992 were down by 80 percent, according to General James Clapper of the Pentagon. Clapper describes the military capabilities of the Commonwealth states as in "profound decline," while Robert Gates, director of the CIA, told the U.S. Senate that the Soviet military threat "has all but disappeared for the forseeable future."[40] In the past decades the United States and its allies have spent literally trillions of dollars to stop Soviet aggression. Talbott observes that, having stopped the former Soviet Union from blowing up the world, for a fraction of the cost we can now help prevent it from blowing up itself, with all the disastrous consequences that would have for the entire world.[41] A *Washington Post* editorial puts the question even more forcibly: "The question for the United States, having spent many hundreds of billions of dollars over the years to defend itself from the Soviet Union, is whether it is willing to invest a very small fraction of that amount in the friendship and prosperity of the former Soviet republics now set free."[42] The peace dividend needs to be reinvested to insure the success of the freedom and democracy that military expenditures sought to obtain for an entire generation.

The domino effect

Nixon has urged another reason why the time has come to help Russia. Russia, as the inheritor of all the political clout that resided in the former union, will set the pace of reform in other republics. When other republics meet the conditions that Russia has (democratic elections, minority rights, and free market reform), we should help them, but only then and not sooner. Supporting Yeltsin now in tangible and sizable ways will encourage other republics to follow

40. Elaine Sciolino, "Soviet Threat Over, Intelligence Chiefs Assure Senators," *IHT,* January 23, 1992, p. 4.

41. Talbott, "State That Deserved to Die."

42. "Russia Can Make It," *IHT,* January 6, 1992, p. 4.

suit. "By assisting Yeltsin's government, we will create an incentive for reform elsewhere," and in so doing, "Russia will lead not by force of its arms but by force of its example."[43] The converse of this logic is also true: If reform in Russia fails, it seems highly unlikely that it will succeed in other republics. This is particularly true given the relative size and importance of the Russian economy (about 65 percent of the GNP of the former USSR, compared to the other former republics). Russia, for example, is the main supplier of oil, gas, and minerals to the other republics.

Historical analogies past and present

After World War II the United States invested millions of dollars to insure the successful reconstruction of the nations of Japan and Germany (the Marshall Plan). Similarly, we extended substantial aid to Poland (to stabilize its weak currency, the *zloty*) and other Eastern European nations in the wake of democratic reforms that exploded there with the fall of the Berlin Wall in 1989. Poland still faces economic struggles, but by most accounts Western investment there has made an essential difference in terms of increased living standards and political stability. After the Persian Gulf War we rightly found the necessary resources to feed and house the Kurds. How can we do less now with regard to what was formerly the largest country on earth, a nation rich in natural resources that has a greater capacity for future self-sufficiency than many countries?

An open market

Gennadi Burbulis, Yeltsin's number two man, offers a final reason the West might consider helping the former Soviet Union, and it consists in a positive rather than negative form of self-interest. Burbulis appeals to the capitalistic potential of his country: "So far we have in Russia a colossal and to a large extent empty market, a very low level of consumption and entire lines of modern western goods that are simply unknown to our people. For instance, there are millions of people living in Moscow, and there is not one dishwasher. Our people simply have no idea what one is. Such goods and services would obviously sell. So there can only be one conclusion: Come,

43. Nixon, "Time Has Come."

make them and sell them."[44] Foreign investment in Russia is not only good for Russia but good for the United States. Creating more jobs for Americans requires finding new markets for our products, especially in the crucial area of exports. There remain only two large, untapped markets in the world now, the former USSR and China, and only the former has moved decisively toward political democracy and a free market.

In these early stages the risk of entering the Russian market are clearly great and shrouded with complexities, but a large number of Western corporations have already started business ventures in the former republics. On January 23, 1991, Yeltsin lifted all import restrictions and customs tariffs in order to stimulate foreign investment. He has urged local and regional authorities to speed up privatization. For the republics, passing on the benefits of the free market system, like lower prices due to competition and economic self-determination through profit incentives, will reap the by-product of political stability. From the Western perspective, greater international investment will hasten the opening up of an enormous but untapped market that otherwise could revert to xenophobic bureaucrats determined to unseat Yeltsin and reverse his radical reforms.

Conclusion

The West must offer a broad variety of helps in the coming decades if Russia is to transcend its abacus-type economy. Membership in the International Monetary Fund and World Bank is only a beginning. Nixon has urged creating an organization to spearhead relief efforts, accelerating aid to agricultural sectors, establishing "enterprise funds" for republics who follow in the footsteps of Russia's radical measures, and expanding scientific and educational exchange programs. Given the historically pathetic weakness of the ruble, making the Russian currency truly convertible is important. Deferral of payments on Russia's foreign debt will release limited monies for domestic urgencies. Transforming the enormous military-industrial complex into civil manufacturing must be a top priority.

44. Burbulis, "Help Russia."

Private initiatives, both large and small, can make a significant impact, for the government cannot solve all the problems in the former Soviet Union. We need to think globally but act locally. Let me speak from our own personal experience. At the English-speaking international church we attend in Moscow, people started a food-sharing program. We employed the services of a Russian restaurant that purchased its food locally and prepared the meals. Local government agencies supplied a list of needy pensioners in our district who could benefit from the program. These people were presented free vouchers that entitled them to one hot meal per day at the cafe. Volunteers from our church greeted the people who came, visited with them, served the food, cleared the tables, and so on. The first cafe worked so well that the church contracted the services of a second one, then a third one. By the winter of 1992 the church was providing nearly 1,000 hot meals per day, six days a week, to needy elderly people in Moscow. Solicitations from churches in the West soon created a $60,000 reserve of funds, an enormous sum for the purposes intended when converted into rubles, set aside exclusively for the project. At this writing, in addition to running the three restaurants, our church was helping a local Russian church learn to operate another restaurant based on the model we used, paying for the costs with funds from our church. Skeptics might say that such an effort does not make a difference, but that is not true. It makes a tremendous impact on those 1,000 pensioners each day, and probably an even greater impact on the volunteers who come to serve. Through creativity and generosity Western Christian organizations can lead the way in helping Russia to help itself and to secure its place in the politically and economically free world. Only then will the Russian economy move beyond the age of the abacus.

4

The Party Is Over:
Politics

Dear countrymen and townsfolk, in view of the situation
that has developed and the formation of the Commonwealth of Independent States, I cease work as the President of the Union of Soviet Socialist Republics. I am making this decision out of consideration of principle. I firmly
supported the independence and sovereignty of the
republics. But at the same time I supported the preservation of the federal state and the country's integrity. Nevertheless, events took a different turn. The predominant
policy was to dismember the country and break up the
state, with which I cannot agree.

　　　　　　　　　　　　—Mikhail Sergeyevich Gorbachev
　　　　　　　　　　　　December 25, 1991[1]

Introduction

On November 10, 1982, when Leonid Ilyich Brezhnev died in
office at the age of seventy-six after eighteen years as the general
secretary of the Communist party, although no one at that time

1. For the complete text of Gorbachev's resignation speech, see Appendix A.

could have fathomed it, Russian politics entered a time warp that in less than three years would alter its once predictable landscape beyond recognition. As if a premonitory symbol of events to follow, Yuri Andropov, former head of the KGB, followed Brezhnev and died only fifteen months later (February 9, 1984). Seventy-year-old Konstantin Chernenko, who succeeded Andropov and was a throwback to the older days of Brezhnev's intransigent bureaucracy, passed across the Soviet stage even more quickly, dying on March 10, 1985. With his death and the subsequent rise to power of Mikhail Sergeyevich Gorbachev, the country's first general secretary to be born after the Bolshevik Revolution, Soviet politics embarked on a roller coaster ride that has not yet ended.

Born in 1931, at the height of Stalin's collectivist purges that killed millions of people, Gorbachev grew up as a country bumpkin outside the tiny village of Privolnoye in the Caucasus region of Stavropol, 800 miles south of Moscow's seat of political power. An only child, his journey from his family's two-room mud brick house that had no running water, to his rise to world power in the spring of 1985, evokes comparisons to America's Abraham Lincoln.[2] Gorbachev redefined Soviet politics beyond anyone's wildest imagination, and after his unceremonious twelve-minute resignation speech, at a farewell party the next day in Moscow's luxurious Oktyabar Hotel, he assured followers that he was not leaving the political scene but that in fact he had "big plans." Even as he spoke, however, the red, blue, and white flag of the Russian Republic supplanted the Soviet's familiar red flag with yellow star, hammer, and sickle atop the Kremlin, and the new commander-in-chief Boris Yeltsin ordered Gorbachev and his family to vacate his Kremlin office and government dacha within twenty-four hours. Gorbachev had become a pensioner.

Such are the paradoxes and contradictions of Russian politics. The drama that began with the prelude of the deaths of Brezhnev, Andropov, and Chernenko, and ended its first act with the reign of Gorbachev, remains an unfinished story. What the geometry of Russian politics will look like with the next turn of the kaleidescope by Yeltsin is anybody's guess.

---

2. Hedrick Smith makes this comparison in his book *The New Russians,* p. 32.

Some attempt, however, can be made to map the new political terrain. Already we can plot the removal of old landmarks by the presence of new ones. Glasnost has heralded a new political psychology and spawned a plethora of "democratic" movements and parties, all of which are haunted by lingering ghosts of the near and distant communist past. Some of these ghosts are no more frightening than Casper; others are downright menacing. The former country's enormous but beleaguered army casts about for a paycheck now that its state-employer has vanished. Secondary and higher education, long the bastion of ideological indoctrination, augurs changes both good and bad. All in all, Gorbachev was right, perhaps even more so than he himself knew: Events in Russian politics have taken a "different turn."

A Genie Unleashed: Glasnost and the New Criticism

Glasnost Ends Samizdat

Russia has long been home to some of the world's greatest dissident literature. Author Alexander Solzhenitsyn and physicist Andrei Sakharov, both Nobel laureates, are only two of the better known names familiar to American readers. But the *samizdat* (literally, "self-published") literature from the underground intelligentsia, literature secretly produced and distributed and punishable as anti-communistic propaganda, has become a relic of the political past. On December 16, 1986, Gorbachev telephoned Sakharov in Gorky to tell him he had dropped the seven-year ban against him and that he would be released (he died in 1989). Exiled to the United States since 1974, Solzhenitsyn, having had the criminal charges against him dropped in 1991, has announced that he will return to his homeland after he finishes his current writing project. Glasnost, meaning to make open, public, or frank, has made dissent and criticism not only possible but fashionable to an extreme. Censorship itself has been censured in contemporary Russia.

Overview of Glasnost

In his 1987 book *Perestroika: New Thinking for Our Country and the World,* Gorbachev described glasnost as an absolutely necessary precondition for his program of democratization and economic restructuring. "We need glasnost as we need the air. . . . There is no democracy, nor can there be, without glasnost." Noting that the public had acquired a "taste for glasnost," he urged that openness and debate be applied comprehensively to every sector of society. Although he knew full well that some in the former Soviet Union still resisted the new policy, Gorbachev insisted that "we will do all in our power to prevent anyone from either suppressing criticism or sidestepping it. Criticism is a bitter medicine, but the ills that plague society make it a necessity. You make a wry face, but you swallow it."[3]

Beyond Gorbachev's personal policy, the 19th All-Union Conference of the Communist party of the Soviet Union (July 1988) astonished Muscovites; its boisterous televised sessions revealed it to be an incarnation of the spirit of criticism carried to an extreme. Political analysts have referred to that July Congress as a political shock treatment, a brawl, a raucous political debate, a cross between a revival and a "freewheeling town meeting." Gorbachev was criticized from the floor; journalists accused Party members of being criminals; speakers urged the dissolution of government ministries; Politburo members were called on to resign; and, in a grand finale of sorts, Boris Yeltsin, whom Gorbachev had ousted from the Politburo only a few months earlier for his radical criticisms and had denounced in his closing conference speech, and Yegor Ligachev, an old-line conservative, locked horns in a free-for-all verbal assault.[4] In the understatement of the conference, made in his closing speech, Gorbachev observed that "The Palace of Congresses has not witnessed such a discussion before, comrades, and I don't think I'll be transgressing against the truth if I say that nothing like it has occurred in our country for nearly the last sixty years."[5]

In the aftermath, the conference issued a series of six resolutions, one of which dealt exclusively with glasnost. That six-page resolution describes glasnost as "one of [the Party's] most crucial political objectives" and its "consistent extension an indispensable condition for expressing the democratic essence of the socialist system." Crit-

3. Mikhail Gorbachev, *Perestroika: New Thinking for Our Country and for the World* (New York: Harper and Row, 1988), pp. 61–66.
4. Cf. Smith, *New Russians,* pp. 116–20.
5. Gorbachev, *Perestroika,* p. 244.

ical dialogue remained a "crucial condition" that had to be applied to "all spheres of life" if the program of perestroika was to succeed. While some tried to resist, block, and suppress the new openness, the Party resolution argued that glasnost had "wholly justified itself, and that it should be promoted in every way in the future."[6] Just what Gorbachev had wrought, and the 19th Congress had emulated, and the political power they together unleashed, continues to unfold at every level of present-day Russia.

General Examples of Glasnost

A university colleague of mine judges a newspaper he does not like as "vulgar anticommunism." Never mind, it is published weekly in both Russian and English. Cab drivers revile Russian politics in the best fashion of blue-collar Americans. Tengiz Abuladze's 1987 film *Repentance* and Anatoli Rybakov's 1988 novel *Children of the Arbat* are only two of many examples of virulent criticism of Stalin. In 1958 Boris Pasternak won the Nobel Prize for his novel *Dr. Zhivago*, only to be spurned by his government; today his complete works are available in Moscow bookshops. National problems like Chernobyl (the target of the 1988 play *The Sarcophagus* by the journalist Vladimir Gubarev), environmentalism, AIDS, drug abuse, and alcoholism are now the material of newspaper editorials and television talk shows.

Three Particular Examples

From our own experience in Moscow, however, three examples of this new culture of criticism stand out. They illustrate the manner, bizarre in these instances, to which the genie of glasnost has defrocked the saints and desecrated the holy books and shrines of the former Soviet socialism that Gorbachev himself struggled mightily to the end to preserve. Gorbachev intended glasnost to be a means to reform and preserve Soviet socialism; in the end it helped to destroy it.

When Boris Yeltsin emerged from the failed coup of August 1991 as the new leader of Russia, one of the things he had the foresight to do was to seize the vast archives of the Communist party stored in Moscow in order to prevent their deliberate destruction. By some

6. Ibid., "Resolutions of the 19th All-Union Conference of the CPSU," pp. 255–96.

estimates these archives contain over 70 million documents. The wisdom of his decision was vindicated in early 1992. Five months after the coup a publisher of university and research databases in Cambridge, England, Chadwyck-Healey, announced a coup of their own. In late January 1992 they announced that they had reached an agreement with the Russian government to microfilm and subsequently make available for purchase the entire Party archives (except for Lenin's file), in turn paying the government royalties on the sale of the materials. The first portion of the materials (more than 300,000 documents) scheduled for release in the fall of 1992 includes meticulously kept Communist party files collected on major leaders of the Bolshevik Revolution, including personal correspondence, police reports, and biographical descriptions of Leon Trotsky, Vyacheslav M. Molotov, Andrei A. Zhdanov, and other close associates of Lenin. Historian Jana Howlett of Cambridge University, who has served as intermediary between the Russian government and Chadwyck-Healey, notes that "the information in these files puts flesh on major historical figures about whom we have really known very little until now." Scholars have hailed the newly available archives as one of the greatest untapped resources of twentieth-century history and a veritable documentary of Soviet communism.[7]

Five weeks after the Bolshevik Revolution, on December 7, 1917, Lenin founded the Soviet secret police, the "All Russia Extraordinary Commission for the Struggle Against Counter-Revolution and Sabotage"— or the *Cheka*, as it was known by its Russian acronym. The *Cheka*, which was actually the precursor to the KGB, was known by all to be "the punishing sword of the revolution" that was above any and all laws. "Iron" Felix Dzerzhinski (1877–1926), the first leader of the terrorist group, insured that the new revolution would be protected against any internal detractors, announcing his creed to his new employer: "Do not believe that I seek revolutionary forms of justice at this point. We are engaged today in hand-to-hand combat, to the death, to the end! I propose, I demand, the revolutionary organization of annihilation against all counterrevolutionaries."[8]

---

7. William E. Schmidt, "Soviet Party Archives to Be Released," *IHT,* January 23, 1992, p. 4.
8. Cited by Mikhail Heller and Aleksandr M. Nekrich, *Utopia in Power: The History of the Soviet Union from 1917 to the Present* (New York: Summit Books, 1986), p. 54.

True to his word, Party members suspected of any signs of dissent suffered brutal terror. When Stalin died in office in 1953, the *Cheka* was reorganized under a new name, the "Committee of State Security" or KGB, which at its height by some estimates had upwards of 100,000 career officers who oversaw the country's espionage, surveillance, and intelligence-gathering efforts.

Today the KGB no longer exists.[9] One of the first icons to tumble from the tremors of the August coup was a statue of Dzerzhinski himself in front of the KGB headquarters. On October 24, 1991, Gorbachev had signed a decree to dissolve the "state within the State" as the KGB was known, which decree the state council approved. A month later, on November 26, 1991, Yeltsin signed a decree "On Transfering the RSFSR State Security Committee into a Federal Security Agency." Then, on December 19, 1991, Yeltsin moved to establish a ministry of security and internal affairs, a move that would have merged part of the old KGB with the Russian ministry of internal affairs to create a new superintelligence agency. On January 14, 1992, however, the Russian constitutional court unanimously ruled the decree unconstitutional, and Yeltsin rescinded his decree, a move hailed by Westerners who insist on facilitating a substantial and not merely cosmetic deconstruction of the KGB.

In a bizarre twist of glasnost, the secret-bound KGB now seeks to turn its closure into a windfall of capitalist profits by reopening its doors for a much different purpose. Every Tuesday and Thursday at 10 A.M., for a mere $30, people can take a three-hour tour of "Moscow's most notorious building," the KGB headquarters in former Dzerzhinski Square. Visitors receive a historical review, albeit a closely-controlled and highly sanitized one, of the former organization (KGB agents who carried out Stalin's purges were "just car-

---

9. This statement must be qualified. Some analysts are quite skeptical about the reputed abolition of the KGB. In a long news analysis Yevgeniya Albats argues that the changes are no more than cosmetic, a mere facelift, and that in fact "practically nothing" has changed at the KGB except for some nomenclature and personnel. The organization "lives on and operates under the same lawlessness." See "KGB—Substantive Changes?" *MN*, January 12–19, 1992, p. 5. Cf. too J. Michael Walker, "The KGB Isn't Dead," *WSJE*, January 28, 1992, who suggests that the same people and structures are still very much entrenched, only under a new name; David Wise, "Closing Down the KGB," *New York Times Magazine*, November 24(?), 1991.

rying out orders"), including oddities like invisible ink, poison cap-
sules, bullet-firing pens, photographs of American agents caught
with their Soviet contacts, a snoop into Dzerzhinski's personal office
(later occupied by Yuri Andropov), and the new KGB gift shop.
Photographs are not allowed, but according to Vladimir Ivlyov,
coordinator of the Intourist project, there is a good reason: Camera-
happy tourists would be less likely to buy the KGB's postcards.
Indeed, for an extra fee, tourists can have their picture taken in front
of a bust of Iron Felix in one of the building's exquisite halls.[10]

Glasnost has not only opened up the shrines and holy books of the
communist past for profit and public consumption; it has even
defrocked its patron saints Marx and Engels. Like those named after
Dzerzhinski, Moscow streets, squares, and metro stations named
after Marx have had their names changed, but in the latter's case
the ignominy goes further. In the wake of the 1917 Revolution the
Bolsheviks confiscated an elegant eighteenth-century Moscow mansion that now stands behind the Pushkin Fine Arts Museum in the
center of Moscow. In 1921 the Central Committee designated it as
the "Institute of Marxism-Leninism," and until recently it housed a
museum dedicated to Marx and Engels. Only one example of the
enormous real estate holdings owned by the Party that Yeltsin's Russian government reclaimed by fiat after the coup, in a recent decision
by the Moscow city council, the mansion was returned to the Union
of the Descendants of the Russian Nobility, who intend to restore the
nearly dilapidated structure to its former splendor within a few years.
For now, until the transaction is completed, both the director of the
former communist museum, Vasily Kuznetsov, and the staff of the
Nobility Union, share the building in a sign of the changes glasnost
has wrought.

An Enlightenment Elixir

In 1784 Immanuel Kant wrote an essay entitled *Was ist Auf-
klarung?* ("What is Enlightenment?") in which he attempted to define the spirit of his age. Kant admitted that his was not an enlightened age, but an age of enlightenment, of humankind's release or

---

10. Peter Conradi, "KGB Opens Its Doors for Guided Tours," *MG,* January 17, 1992, pp.
1, 11.

freedom from self-incurred tutelage, from a slavery to external authorities fostered by fear and laziness. The antidote to this sickness, wrote Kant, was the development of the faculty of critical and independent inquiry, the audacity to think for one's self—*sapere aude!*— Have courage to use your own understanding! Without ever having experienced the Renaissance, the Reformation, or the Enlightenment, at least not in the manner and to the extent that the West did, it is as if glasnost's elixir of this Enlightenment spirit was ingested by the entire former Soviet Union. As Gorbachev observed in his book *Perestroika,* taking medicine is sometimes unpleasant, but even when it is unpleasant it can bring healing.

My own experience of life and work on the faculty of philosophy at Moscow State University, and as a visitor to a dozen other Soviet cities and universities, attests to the salutary impact of glasnost's new culture of criticism. It still startles me to ponder that an evangelical theologian like myself could teach in a department that only a few years ago was called the department of Scientific Atheism. In my lectures and discussions with undergraduate and graduate students from nearly all of the republics, professors, department chairs, deans, vice rectors, scholars such as the director of the Lenin Library, and dorm neighbors, I can say that we were not merely tolerated but warmly received. Never once were we restricted in any sense. I was allowed to teach any course I chose, and present whatever material I felt appropriate. People were eager to encounter a Westerner and to make up for seven decades of intellectual repression. Now unleashed, the genie of glasnost has begotten a new political psychology in the former Soviet Union. *Samizdat* and the literature of dissent, having won the freedom it fought so long to obtain, will never be the same.

Defining Democracy: A Cacophony of Voices

The Rise of Political Parties

The former one-party nation will never be the same. Glasnost's lonely voices of dissent, who heretofore could only cry from their exilic deserts, have now become heralds shouting from the mountain tops. Open criticism not only vanquished the hegemony of the

Communist party; it gave rise to a plethora of new political parties. If the party is over for the former Communists of the vanished Soviet Union, a new sort of party of democracy has begun in Russia. The various democratic movement groups that joined together to sweep Yeltsin into office as the president of Russia in the country's first free presidential election, and four months later rallied at the Russian White House to defeat right-wing conservative forces in the failed coup, now exist as a loose, fragile and fractious alliance. The sad but ironic truth is that Russia's most brazen reformer, Yeltsin, is alienated from the very democratic movement that ushered him into power. In December 1991 at the third congress of the Democratic party of Russia, the country's largest democratic party, member Stanislav Fyodorov put it bluntly: "We are just learning democracy."[11]

At present Yeltsin's administration has no party affiliation, and consequently there is no "ruling party" in Russia. Would-be "opposition groups" abound, although they complain that Yeltsin has turned a deaf ear to them. The Soviet Union's one-party system gave way to a multiparty system on January 2, 1991, when registered political parties and associations were allowed. Today over 140 political groups, both registered and unregistered, exercise the privilege of party politics bestowed on them by glasnost (see Appendix B for a complete list). They range from right-wing groups like the Orthodox Constitutional Monarchy party, founded May 19, 1990 (birthday of Tsar Nicholas II), which intends to unite the Orthodox Church, the army, and the KGB under a constitutional monarchy, and the Neo-Stalinist Russian Communist party, which favors Russian imperialism; to left-wing reform-minded groups like the Confederation of Anarcho-Syndicalists, which sanctions the total abolition of the state. Although outlawed by Yeltsin, various communist parties also continue to operate, like the Marxist Platform of the Communist party, the United Workers' Front, and the Democratic Platform of the Communist party. We will examine them below.[12] Even the anti-Semitic Pamyat Society has its following. Beyond this cacophony of extremist voices, the following sampler outlines some of the role players, both democratic and communist,

11. David Filipov, "Discord among the Democrats," *MG,* December 13, 1991, p. 7.
12. Cf. "Guide to Soviet Democracy," *The Economist,* May 26, 1990, p. 52.

important and insignificant, jostling for position and influence in Russia's political sweepstakes.[13]

Democratic Party of Russia (DPR). Founded in May 1990, the DPR is the largest registered democratic party, with about 50,000 members. It has structures set up in most of Russia's regions but no parliamentary group of its own. About a dozen Russian parliament members are DPR members. Nikolai Travkin serves as the current chairman, and urges his party to support Yeltsin conditionally but critically.

Russian Christian Democratic Movement (RCDM). Viktor Aksyuchits of the party's leadership describes his RCDM party as "a neoconservative party similar to the US Republican Party or the British Tories."[14] Founded in the spring of 1990, this right-wing movement has 15,000 members and representative offices in all of Russia's republics. It opposes Yeltsin's economic policies and the government (but not Yeltsin himself), which it believes are making Russia dependent on Western capitalism.

The Constitutional Democrats. Along with the first two groups, the Cadets form the so-called National Accord Bloc. Founded in June 1991, the party has 6,000 members in Russia, Ukraine, Moldavia, Kazakhstan, and Byelorussia. Its agenda is to build a democratic society and a market economy through privatization, abolition of monopolies, and deregulation. In January 1992 the party announced its opposition to the Yeltsin government.

Republican Party of the Russian Federation (RPRF). A splinter group from the Democratic Platform in the CPSU, the RPRF was founded in November 1990 and has about nine members in the Russian parliament. It claims a membership of 15,000. Its platform is similar to that of the Social Democratic party.

Social Democratic Party of Russia (SDPR). A center-left party with about 5,000 members in 106 regions, the SDPR was begun in May 1990. It has connections with social democratic parties in Western Europe. SDPR member Alexander Shokin was appointed

---

13. Summaries taken from "Guide to Soviet Democracy" (ibid.); Len Karpinsky, "The Parties and Russian Reform," *MN*, January 26–February 2, 1992, p. 8; and Tass news agency's Stenographic Bulletin Service of Principal Political Parties as of April 1992.

14. Fillipov, "Discord."

minister of labor. Currently it has no instituted chairman, although some of its leaders include Oleg Rumyantsev, Leonid Volkov, and Boris Orlov. Along with the Republican party and the Democratic party, it is one of the three largest noncommunist parties in Russia.

Free Russia People's Party (FRPP). This party is an off-shoot of the Communists for Democracy Movement that spurned the CPSU after the failed August coup. At its first congress on October 26–27, 1991, the FRPP had a membership of 100,000 in 62 regions, most of whom were communists who left the CPSU after the failed coup. About 100 deputies in the Russian parliament identify with the FRPP. Alexander Rutskoi, Russia's vice president who has openly critcized Yeltsin for his policies of "economic genocide," is the party's chairman. Some analysts point to the FRPP as "the most effective tool for the organizational and ideological reunification of centrist communists in Russia."[15]

Socialist Party of Working People (SPWP). Formed in December 1991, this newcomer enrolls 6,000 members in 65 regional organizations. In parliament it has 24 deputies, mainly from the Communists of Russia group. Among the party's seven co-chairmen are Anatoly Denisov, cosmonaut Vitaly Sevastyanov, and historian Roy Medvedev. Cited as a "revivalist" communist group, they intend to restore the CPSU with only cosmetic changes in its doctrine and structure. As the ideological successors to the Communist party, they consider Russia's economic reforms to be socially unjust and economically ineffective.

Party of Free Labor (PFL). Established in December 1990 this group has no representation in parliament. It claims to represent the "owners of capital goods and the owners of labor power." The PFL belongs to the Freedom and Dignity liberal bloc. It stands for political pluralism, direct presidential elections, and equality of all types of ownership. Igor Korovikov is its chairman.

Peasant Party of Russia (PPR). The key objective of the PPR, which was started in September 1990, is to advocate the rights of peasants in the realm of politics, economics, and society. It supports the abolition of collective farms and state farms, and favors the estab-

15. No author, "Neo-Communist Organizations in Russia," *MN,* January 19–26, 1992, p. 14.

lishment of private property. It claims to represent the interests of the peasantry and all who produce agricultural products. Yuri Chernichenko is its chairman. Affiliated with the Democratic Russia Movement, its membership numbers about 600.

Problems for Democracy

Problems within and among the new parties continue to plague the democratic movement. Most disturbing is a recent analysis that reveals that "more than half the population [of Russia] has no real conception of what democracy is."[16] Boris Grushin argues that it is nothing more than a myth that democracy has taken root in Russia. His poll estimates that nearly 80 percent of Russians have no meaningful idea about the meaning of democracy; when asked to define democracy, people in this group respond with notions of rigid control, the role of a strong leader, anarchic tendencies to do whatever you like, and so on. Only about 20 percent identify elements of genuine democracy like equality, the inalienable right of individuals over the state, observation of constitutional freedoms, the separation of government powers, and so on. Grushin concludes, "this motley picture of present-day consciousness inspires no special optimism."[17] One example of this confusion about the meaning of democracy comes from an article in *Rossiiskaya Gazeta* (December 20, 1991), which argued that criticizing the Yeltsin reform efforts was "one of the greatest threats to democracy." True democracy, of course, promotes rather than discourages such public debate about important issues.

Through no fault of its own the current government inherited the infrastructures of its predecessors, with the result that few avenues for democratic dialogue exist. Another consequence of this inheritance is that representational government is a long way off in contemporary Russia. Perhaps the single greatest criticism voiced against Yeltsin, former Moscow Mayor Gavril Popov, and their administrations, is that they rule by the authoritarian methods of the past. Although Yeltsin and nine parties signed a "Protocol of Agreement" on November 28, 1991, in which they pledged mutual coopera-

16. Boris Grushin, "Democracy as Understood in Modern Russia," *MN,* January 27–February 2, 1992, p. 7.
17. Ibid.

tion, to date Yeltsin has been unable and apparently uninterested in building a coalition of democratic party support. Mikhail Astavyev of the Cadets leadership complains that "some of the so-called democrats in charge of the country right now do things the Communists would have never dared do." He cites the example of a Moscow council chairman who deliberately refused to call a council meeting in order to avoid certain impeachment. Oleg Rumyantsev of the SDPR protests that "the existing administration is a brazen and cynical army of new, aggressive officialdom which is out to capture premises, positions [and] capital."[18]

Nikolai Travkin, leader of the DPR, points to another dilemma, and perhaps the greatest apprehension, faced by all the democratic parties—not democratic factionalism, which has been a genuine inhibitor of progress, but a lurch to the right. "We could easily find ourselves with a dictator like [neonationalist leader Vladimir] Zhirinovsky."[19] To be sure, the legacy of Lenin, and even Stalin, remains an open case in contemporary Russia. Alexei Kiva voiced a similar concern in an essay in the *Moscow News*. According to Kiva, "there are chances of a new totalitarianism during the transitional period as a reaction to the new utopias that peddle Western ways or Slavophilism. . . . The hungry, angry people who see the super-power crumbling together with their imagined well-being would support the concept of a powerful state, national unity or just 'order' over the ideas of western liberalism."[20] When the vice president (Alexander Rustkoi) of the administration heads a communist party and openly criticizes the reform efforts of the president (Yeltsin), potential problems are not far away. By mid-February 1992 Yeltsin had had enough of Rustkoi's criticisms, and so marginalized him by making him head of agriculture. Russia's inability to settle the issue of Lenin's legacy and the rise of neocommunist parties illustrate this point.

In the bitter cold on January 21, 1992, several hundred dedicated communist supporters marched to Lenin's mausoleum in Red Square to commemorate the sixty-eighth anniversary of his death. They carried placards, chanted slogans, denounced the new com-

18. Len Karpinsky, "Parties and Russian Reform."
19. Fillipov, "Discord."
20. Alexei Kiva, "From Perestroika to a Dictatorship?" *MN,* February 5–12, 1992, p. 6.

monwealth, reviled the leaders of reform, and generally glorified the founder of the Soviet state. In fact, the march was organized to protest the rumors that have constantly circulated in Moscow for months that Lenin's body might be removed from the mausoleum and buried with his family in St. Petersburg. Debate exists about Lenin's will and his preference on the matter, and his grand niece has urged a public referendum to determine whether to bury him. When Lenin died in 1924, his followers argued for a month while his body lay in state. Afterwards his body was mummified and entombed in a wooden mausoleum on Red Square, where it rested until the present structure was built in 1930. During the German invasion of 1941 the body was moved to the Urals to protect it, and then returned in 1945. The work-day crowd that Tuesday in late January was much smaller than their regular weekend protests that often draw thousands of people to protest price increases, but it is an example of why people like Travkin and Kiva voice their fears.[21]

Like the democrats, neocommunists have taken advantage of glasnost to form their own parties, as can be seen in groups like the FRPP and the SPWP. Neo-Bolsheviks or orthodox Marxists exemplify the extremist communist elements that still exist in current Russian politics. These groups are far removed from most popular opinion and political forces, but for that very reason their presence troubles people like Travkin and Kiva. Parties in this category vigorously discredit the democracy movement and efforts at reform, and conversely seek to justify the history and practice of the CPSU. The Russian Communist Workers' party and the New Party of Russia's Communists are insignificant groups right now, but the All-Union Communist party of Bolsheviks, led by Nina Andreyeva, held its first congress on November 8, 1991, in St. Petersburg and today claims 35,000 active supporters.[22] These staunch Stalinists vigorously reject current efforts

21. On the debate to bury Lenin, see Thomas Ginsberg, "Communists Mark Lenin's Death," *MG,* January 24, 1992, p. 7; Sergei Razgonov, "How We Shall Bury Lenin," *MN,* September 29–October 6, 1991, p. 7; and "Lenin's Tomb from the Top Down" and "What Is to Be Done with the Mausoleum?" *MN,* October 13–20, 1991, pp. 2–3. In Razgonov's article an opinion poll indicated that 66 percent of the respondents felt like the mausoleum should remain if Lenin's body is buried; only 20 percent wanted to remove it; 14 percent did not know.

22. See "Neo-Communist Organizations in Russia."

to democratize society, and their kin can be seen demonstrating to that end almost any weekend in Red Square.

Conclusion: Cautious Optimism

Westerners can rejoice in the new beginnings of democracy that have resulted from glasnost. The current political scene—with dozens of "democratic" parties voicing their concerns, building their coalitions, badgering Yeltsin to listen, trying to represent views of the people, vigilantly resisting a throwback to the autocratic past—represents a monumental improvement over the past. But at times it seems like the problems like those just mentioned overshadow the successes.

Some of the major components of the CIS itself remained undefined—ministerial committees that are supposed to coordinate the republics, policy to guide the so-called economic space the republics agreed on, citizenship, and security of borders. Over fifty "agreements" have been signed by the eleven member states (all of the old republics minus the three Baltic states and Georgia), but leaders complain that few of them have been implemented. Few people even agree on the purpose of the commonwealth, and pressure has mounted to abandon it altogether. One senior official from the Bush administration admitted that "there's no real Commonwealth in any functioning sense in terms of economic policy. It isn't really there."[23]

Henry Kissinger rightly notes that the appellation "democracy" to republics of the former Soviet Union is premature, and in some instances little more than a "courtesy title that reflects a hope rather than a record. . . . [I]t would be a mistake to treat anti-Stalinism as a fundamental conversion to democracy. Recent events in several of the republics leave little doubt that the lesson of democracy in a country with few democratic traditions remains incomplete." Further, if the United States does not give "equal time" to the other republics, and concentrates only on Russia, it might unwittingly contribute to what Kissinger calls a "dangerous recentralization" of power in Moscow, thus undermining genuine democratization in the former republics.[24]

23. Doyle McManus and Douglas Jehl, "Washington Fears CIS Doomed to Fail," *NF*, February 28, 1992. Cf. Michael Parks, "Commonwealth Sows Seeds of Dissolution," *NF*, March 23, 1992.

Thus, the jury is certainly still out and any final celebration of democracy's ultimate triumph in Russia is certainly premature.

But regardless of where on the spectrum a political party lies, the ultimate litmus test they now face is not just merely to insure their own survival in a field of 140 parties, but to demonstrate how they will heal the many open wounds now festering in the country. In other words, although they all provide different answers and prescribe different medicines, all the parties face the same set of national problems and symptoms. In the previous chapter we examined the threat of economic chaos. In the chapter that follows we will focus on religion. In the remainder of this chapter we will look at two examples of the very different sorts of challenges that the new parties face: the former Soviet Union's military complex, and changes wrought in the realm of education.

A Beleaguered Military: New Problems for Potential Peace

Introduction

For the last sixty years or so in the former Soviet Union November 7 has marked an important celebration of the Bolshevik Revolution, in which an annual parade in Moscow's Red Square featured a regal display of the country's impressive military hardware. In November 1991, both the parade and the official holiday were discontinued for the first time. In Baku, Azerbaijan, an enormous monument to the Soviet's 36th Army that "liberated" the city was removed while I visited there in April 1992. Today the Soviet army, once the largest in the world by some measures, is in disarray, and the greater military meltdown of the former Soviet troops and nuclear arsenals offers both a tremendous threat to and an unprecedented opportunity for world peace.

New Problems

The proliferation of Soviet nuclear technology and resources poses a major threat to world peace. With battered economies that sorely

---

24. Henry Kissinger, "Risks of Using Democracy as a Guide," *NF,* January 28, 1992.

lack hard currency, the former Soviet republics have already had opportunities to sell their wares. Two recent examples illustrate the ominous possibilities that now exist.

In the Central Asian republic of Tajikistan, bordering Afghanistan and Pakistan, large uranium mines and enrichment plants now come under control of the government. In fact, the Soviet's first atomic bomb was made with uranium from Tajikistan. With its fledgling economy, the export of uranium is a lucrative and almost irresistible opportunity for the new country. In a sensational news article published by *Narodnaya Gazeta,* a newspaper that has traditionally expressed the views of the Tajikistan government, it was reported that the possible sale of uranium to Libya was being discussed by the two governments. Another possibility mentioned was the development of a consortium with wealthy Arab states to develop the uranium deposits. This article appeared the day that a delegation from Libya left Tajikistan's capital city of Dushanbe after having signed a letter of intent to establish "good-neighbour relations" between the two countries. Government authorities refused to comment on the article about the sale or development of Tajikistan's uranium.[25] About two weeks later, in February 1992, U.S. Secretary of State James Baker met with Rakhmon Nabiyev, then the president of Tajikistan. Nabiyev denied the reports regarding sales of uranium to Libya, saying, "as far as the uranium is concerned, I must say that the press is ahead of events. Tajikistan has never sold and will never sell uranium to other important countries."[26] Since Nabiyev was a communist holdover brought out of retirement to run for president against Islamic fundamentalists, and since he was ousted by Muslim opposition forces (May 1992), Western analysts worry about the significance of the assurances. Neighboring Turkmenistan and Uzbekistan likewise have rich uranium deposits and have already been visited by high-ranking delegates from Libya and Iran.

In a similar nuclear nightmare scenario the Russian foreign ministry has confirmed that substantial arms sales to Iran have taken place. This spread of Soviet nuclear resources to the Islamic world,

25. Asal Azamova, "Uranium for Islamic Bomb?" *MN,* January 19–26, 1992.

26. Thomas Friedman, "Promise to Baker: Tajikistan Will Curb Exports of Uranium," *IHT,* February 14, 1992, p. 2.

paramilitary groups, and even terrorists, unnerves Western analysts, and well it should. The threat is a real one and not merely potential as the following incidents demonstrate.

Besides the sale of uranium to other nations, there is also the problem of the former Soviet Union's enormous "army" of trained scientists and engineers (the largest in the world and twice as many as in the United States). An estimated 5,000 nuclear scientists have the background and training to develop and build nuclear weapons (some estimates suggest 100,000 worked in weapons manufacturing). Many of these scientists, like the rest of their fellow citizens, struggle simply to survive. Their institutes face massive cutbacks in government subsidies. They endure poor scientific working conditions. One brilliant historian friend of mine, for example, cannot carry out his research as he would like because he must work extra jobs to make ends meet. Another scientist friend in Moscow, who was traveling to Germany for a year of research (and hoping never to return), remarked to me one day that "in two years there will not be any scientists in Russia." Of course, he was exaggerating, but his prognosis pointed to a real problem, and one that has special ramifications for the nuclear community.

In a disturbing revelation in early 1992 Vyacheslav Rozanov, deputy chief of Moscow's thermonuclear department at Kurchatov Institute of Atomic Energy, the former country's top nuclear research center, confirmed that Libya had offered at least two of the institute's nuclear scientists high-paying jobs, reputedly for work in peaceful nuclear research. The scientists declined the jobs, but Rozanov admitted that higher offers might prove hard to resist (Libya had offered the scientists $2,000 a month). In a similar but unconfirmed story, an Egyptian newspaper, *Al Watan al Arabi*, reported that Iran had hired fifty former Soviet nuclear scientists and purchased three nuclear weapons for more than $150 million. Boris M. Murashkin, chairman of a newly created Union of Designers of Nuclear Warheads, put it bluntly when he said, "more than anything else, I fear that our nuclear arms technology will fall into the hands of some fanatic."[27] Murashkin rejects the reassurances of some that no scientists are considering offers from renegade nations, and he says it is "reckless" to ignore

27. Elizabeth Shogren, "Ex-Soviet Atomic Scientists Speak Out," *NF,* March 25, 1992.

the possibility. In fact, he is right. Yuri Osipov, president of the Russian Academy of Science, reports that 500 members of the academy have already left for jobs in the West.[28]

At least some initial efforts are being made to provide these orphaned scientists with good living conditions and challenging work. American officials have met with fifty top nuclear scientists of the former Soviet Union at Chelyabinsk-70, one of two major top-secret nuclear complexes in the country. The scientists appealed to Secretary of State James Baker for help, reminded him of the deplorable conditions and tempting offers they faced, presented him with a memorandum outlining creative alternatives to employ the scientists, and assured him that most scientists wanted to use their expertise in constructive ways. According to the chief scientist of Chelyabinsk, Yevgeni N. Avrorin, "what was used for war purposes must now be used for peace."[29] Weeks after Baker's meeting with the scientists at Chelyabinsk, it was announced that $100 million had been pledged to establish the International Science and Technology Center in Moscow and Ukraine ($25 million from the United States, the remainder from Japan and the European Community). The center will employ 2,000 to 3,000 ex-Soviet scientists and give grants in an effort to redirect the talents of the scientists and minimize the possibility that they will sell their skills to other nations.[30]

Related to the sale of nuclear resources like uranium and scientists, there is the threat of the command and control of the 27,000 nuclear warheads in the former Soviet Union that still reside in the independent states of Russia, Ukraine, Byelorussia, and Kazakhstan (not to mention the nonstrategic and battlefield weapons dispersed throughout all fifteen former republics). The latter three nations have indicated a desire to be nuclear-free, and after Gorbachev resigned Yeltsin made it a big point to declare that he alone was in control of the so-called nuclear button and that the warheads were safe. The U.S. Congress even appropriated $400 million to help dismantle the arsenal.

28. Stephen Budiansky, "A Scientific Bazaar," *US News and World Report,* May 4, 1992, p. 60.

29. David Hoffman, "Baker Assures Elite of Ex-Soviet Scientists," *IHT,* February 15–16, 1992, pp. 1, 4.

30. Joanne Levine, "Science Center Aims to Plug Brain Drain," *MT,* May 6, 1992, p. 3.

But in late December 1991, General Yuri Gusev, responsible for central space armaments, acknowledged that on December 20, 1991, two intercontinental ballistic missiles—a Soviet SS-19 with the ability to carry six nuclear warheads, and an SS-18 with the ability to carry ten warheads—were fired from Kazakhstan without the knowledge of Kazakh officials. Kazakh authorities indicated that their fledgling state did not have the technological capability to control flights from its launch sites in Tyuratam. Although the launch was only a test, and one that had been scheduled for months, it violated the START treaty that was signed between the United States and the former Soviet Union on July 31, 1991.

At issue here is the matter of command and control, or what some call the threat of "loose nukes." With China already possessing nuclear weapons, India and Pakistan in the forefront of "threshold nations" close to possession of them, and nations like Libya, Iraq, and Iran buying their way into the nuclear club, one columnist rightly refers to the sinister threat of a "nuclear neighborhood" in Central Asia. David Howell warns that "a failure now to halt the proliferation of nuclear powers among the Central Asian successor states would be the most costly defeat for the guardians of world peace since the 1930s, perhaps of all time."[31] In the spring of 1992, the Ukraine announced that it had stopped shipping its tactical nuclear weapons to Russia to be dismantled because it feared the dismantling might not take place and that the weapons would fall into the wrong hands. Later it announced that it would honor its previous agreement.

In addition to nuclear proliferation there is the threat of conventional weapons and troops. The former Soviet military, especially the high-ranking officers, has long been an organization of privilege, prestige, and national pride, but now it finds itself orphaned. It no longer has a country to defend or a state to serve. What republic it now defends is even uncertain. From fighting to insure the survival of the former country, today the military fights for its own survival. Veterans from the Afghan war, a war that left a million dead, 2 million wounded, and 5 million refugees (the largest refugee population

31. David Howell, "Central Asia, Where the Neighbors Have Nukes," *WSJE*, January 29, 1992, p. 6.

in the world), struggle with a Vietnam-type bitterness; 370,000 former Soviet troops must be relocated from East Germany. Ethnic hostilities between Ukranians and Russians serving in the same navy have been widely reported. Shorn of their prestige and privilege and suffering moral, financial, and physical humiliation, some fear that the military, one of the last major infrastructures from the former Soviet Union with any potential clout, could follow a new strongman who offers to bring back the older days of glory celebrated each November. So far Yeltsin has managed to gain their confidence, but how long that will last remains to be seen.[32]

As was indicated in an earlier chapter, the disposition of the Black Sea Fleet, which both the Ukraine and Russia claim, threatens the stability of the commonwealth. The Ukraine, Byelorussia, Uzbekistan, Moldavia, and Azerbaijan have all made declarations that they intend to establish their own nationalist armies. Not to be outdone, Yeltsin insisted that if the nations followed through with this threat, Russia too would be "forced" to start its own army. He appointed himself as the acting Russian defense minister, giving himself direct control over most of the former Soviet military. In the spring of 1992, Russia announced that because the CIS could not keep the bulk of the 3.7 million Soviet troops united it would issue a presidential decree creating its own armed forces of about 1.5 million troops. Within two weeks it kept its promise and Yeltsin signed the decree. What would happen to the other 2.2 million troops was not mentioned.[33]

Potentials for Peace

The proliferation of nuclear weapons and the disintegration of the conventional military challenge world peace. But not all the developments in the former Soviet Union spell gloom and doom. Promising new gains have already been made that point toward the possibility of lasting peace between the United States and its former enemy. Top military strategists believe that the former Soviet

---

32. Yuri Teplyakov analyzes this threat in his article "Where Will the Army Go?" *MN,* January 26–February 2, 1992, p. 3.

33. Elizabeth Shogren, "Yeltsin: Russia Will Form Own Army," *NF,* February 13, 1992; *IHT,* May 8, 1992, pp. 1f.

military has now been defanged, and that for the forseeable future it does not pose a threat to the United States. Yeltsin has already made moves regarding Russia's nuclear stockpiles and strategies that give reasons for even greater optimism.

Partly by economic necessity, but also partly by deliberate choice, in early 1992 Yeltsin announced a new Russian peace initiative. Acting in concert with President Bush's State of the Union address of late January in which he announced plans to reduce nuclear arsenals, Yeltsin spoke to a television audience and urged that "nuclear weapons and other means of mass annihilation must be eliminated. Conditions are now ripe for major new steps aimed at arms reductions. We are taking some of them unilaterally, and others on the basis of reciprocity." At another meeting, specific proposals by Yeltsin to the Security Council of the United Nations were directed to just the sorts of threats mentioned above—controls on uranium and the sale and export of nuclear technologies. Yeltsin went on to indicate that he has already initiated a unilateral ten-point program of demilitarization that would reduce conventional and nuclear weapons, cut defense spending, halt production of heavy bombers, eliminate the manufacture of cruise missiles, cut nuclear submarine patrols by 50 percent, reduce ground and air maneuvers, and eliminate more than half of Russia's tactical nuclear weapons. While in October 1991 Gorbachev had announced a major plan to reduce nuclear weaponry, Yeltsin's plan both accelerated the timetable (a 30 percent reduction would be accomplished in three years rather than seven years) and increased the amount of the reductions. If the United States would act reciprocally, Yeltsin said, he was prepared to reduce nuclear arsenals on both sides by 80 percent to 2,000 nuclear warheads each. Using as his principle a "reasonable minimum [nuclear] sufficiency," Yeltsin indicated that the economic savings would be used for civilian needs and economic reforms. Further, in terms of strategy, he publically declared that Russian long-range missiles were no longer targeted at major U.S. cities, and called for a global defense system "from Vancouver to Vladivostok" in which the world's nuclear powers would join together to prevent a nuclear tragedy. In a later speech to the United Nations Conference on Disarmament in Geneva, Yeltsin went even further, urging the world's five nuclear nations to put their weapons on "zero alert."[34] Boris Ivanov of Russia's foreign affairs ministry, an arms control expert who participated in the START talks in Geneva in July 1991, has echoed Yeltsin's posture by proposing the possibility of similar, radical reductions in nuclear stockpiles.[35] How the West responds to these radical proposals, and whether they can be parleyed into concrete peace dividends, remains to be seen.

Education and the Intelligentsia: Old Problems, New Potential

Introduction

As with the military, the realm of education augurs developments both alarming and encouraging. An age-old problem that other places like Hong Kong have faced, brain drain, is emptying the former Soviet Union of some of its best minds at the very time in its history when it needs them the most. Problems of finance and administration also wreak havoc. But the new culture of glasnost has also cast aside old ideologies and opened up new opportunities.

Problems

Ironically, at the same time that glasnost is welcoming home exiled dissidents like Solzhenitsyn, deteriorating conditions and a bleak future provide reasons enough for many Soviet intellectuals to emigrate to places that promise better sustenance and support. When my scientist friend told me that no scientists would be left in Russia in a few years, including himself, he incarnated the documented phenomenon of Soviet brain drain. When I remarked to him that it must be hard for him and his wife (also a Ph.D. engineer) to leave behind all of their friends and relocate in Germany, he startled us by saying that it was not that difficult because many of their friends had already left, and others were looking for the opportunity. The night before they left for Germany I shared a toast of champagne

---

34. Michael Parks, "Yeltsin Ups Ante on Disarmament," *NF,* February 13, 1992.

35. Boris Ivanov, "With a New Russia, Arms Control Can Move Faster," *WSJE,* January 30, 1992, p. 6.

with them in their apartment, and asked his wife how she felt on the eve of their departure. She sat upright in her chair, stuck out her chin, smiled, and gave a vigorous thumbs-up sign.

The problem of brain drain has become acute for a number of reasons. The sheer numbers are now so great that some analysts refer to the exodus as a literal flood. According to Lygia O'Riordan, conductor of the Ensemble XXI in Moscow (the first international orchestra based in Moscow since the Revolution), the Tchaikovsky Conservatory has "literally become a ghost building. Every major professor has left, and the head of practically every faculty has left."[36] Norman Lebrecht reports that in the field of music alone "nearly all of the country's top composers are [now] living abroad," leaving the Russian musical scene decimated.[37] Further, the problem has affected nearly every field—a "veritable Who's Who of Soviet talent" not only in music, but science, literature, math, medicine, law, dance, and even chess.[38] Soviets now in the West report being beseiged by their colleagues who still live in the former Soviet Union. Observers also point out the fact that the brain drain is decimating one of the few bright spots in the former Soviet Union—a rich intellectual culture.

In the past decades the reason for the exodus was obvious—communist repression. But today the primary reason, which finds expression in different forms, is economics. Relaxed travel restrictions make emigration easier now, but bread and butter are still the major motives for leaving. The average salary of about $10 a month in Russia is light years away from what the best and brightest minds of Russia can earn in the West, and for many the lure is understandably too strong to resist. My scientist friend and his wife said they refused to rear their children here. When musicians Dimitri Smirnov and Elena Firsova, a married couple and two of the country's leading composers, relocated in Britain, they cited their inability to feed their children: "Moscow was dangerous for the health of my children," said Firsova. "There was no good food. No meat, no

---

36. Susi Lemay, "Plugging the Brain Drain," *MG*, October 18, 1991, p. 6.
37. Norman Lebrecht, "Musical Exodus from a Troubled Russia," *NF*, January 9, 1992.
38. Margaret Shapiro, "Best Soviet Minds Are Bidding Farewell," *IHT*, November 25, 1991, p. 8.

chicken. For milk, Dimitri went out five times a day. Every two months the children had problems with teeth. Now they have very good health."[39] Physicist Alexei Abrikosov, winner of the prestigious Lenin Prize and a member of the Academy of Science, put it rather bluntly: "If you spend all day trying to get a car fixed and trying to find food, it doesn't stimulate theoretical research."[40] He now works in Chicago. In the first quarter of 1992, for example, the Russian Academy of Science received less than half of the $20 million promised to it by the government.[41] Other intellectuals "emigrate" not to another country but out of the intellectual community and into careers in business. For others the scientific working conditions have deteriorated so much that cutting edge work has become impossible. They have little in the way of equipment and materials; scientific journals are a luxury few libraries and institutes can afford, writers cannot publish because of paper shortages, and doctors who work in unsanitary hospitals have no medicine to prescribe. Others have simply lost their jobs and cannot find new ones that will maximize their talents. Victor Yerofeyev, a writer who now spends about half of his time overseas, aptly summarizes all these variants on the single economic theme: "Life here is so humiliating. All artists have left the country. Either they have emigrated or spend most of their time overseas. The whole level of intellectual life is going down."[42]

General administrative cutbacks and slashed budgets in the wake of economic reform also plague the academy. The prestigious Lenin Library (now renamed the Russian State Library), the largest library in the world with 40 million volumes, provides a case in point. The director of the library, historian Igor Fillipov, remarked to me one day in September 1991 that in the past year or so the library had not made a single acquisition except for perhaps a few bartering deals—no books, journals, newspapers, not anything. In late November 1991 the library closed altogether for six weeks because it could not afford to make health and safety repairs ordered by Moscow city inspectors. Dust levels were two to ten times higher than per-

39. Lebrecht, "Musical Exodus."
40. Shapiro, "Best Soviet Minds," p. 1.
41. Budiansky, "Scientific Bazaar," p. 59.
42. Shapiro, "Best Soviet Minds," p. 1.

mitted, and lighting was so bad that users regularly brought their own bulbs.

From my conversations with the dean of the philosophy faculty and the former vice rector of humanities at Moscow State I know that their jobs have been thrown into a state of confusion by the reform movement. The old system of central command had at least one benefit, that of a clear hierarchy that called the shots. Today that administrative hierarchy is gone, and with it the financial resources it wielded. Formerly funded by the state, which no longer exists, the university must now scramble for hard-to-find resources from the Republic of Russia, and as is so often true in the West, education takes a back seat to commerce and industry. In December 1991, payroll was met only after extensive negotiations with both Gorbachev and Yeltsin. Beginning in January 1992, to cite another example, I did not receive a paycheck because the professor I had replaced the first semester had returned. A line item in the university's new budget for international professors had been eliminated. The sum only amounted to $10 a month (although by Russian standards it was a full professor's salary), and it was a cause of genuine frustration and embarrassment for the dean (he called it "a matter of principle") that I should work and not get paid, but the administrative and financial problems at the university complicated even a simple matter like this. The zeal of the dean and vice rector to treat me with the utmost generosity only embarrassed them and saddened me.

New Potentials

Despite brain drain and administrative and financial nightmares, new potentials for genuine progress now exist as never before not only for Christian ministries but in literally every field.

One cold, rainy day in October 1991, I hopped a cab to go speak at Moscow's Public High School #123. The receptionist at my son's school, a Russian, had asked me if I would speak to her daughter's class on the meaning of Christianity. Of course I obliged, and so on that rainy day I found myself standing before about fifty eager-beaver Russian teenagers, all of whom spoke impeccable English. For the next two hours I explained the gospel, answered questions, dialogued with teachers, and met with the school's headmaster. When

I was introduced, and before I had spoken a word, the teacher exclaimed to the class how wonderful it was that I was there, and that she was sure that this was only the first of many visits there by me. When I had finished, in keeping with a delightful Russian tradition, they presented me with a large bouquet of flowers. Later the headmaster assured me that he and his school were "at my disposal" and that they would welcome me to help them in whatever ways I might offer.

What is most remarkable about this story is that today in the former Soviet Union it is not at all unusual. Several friends of mine in Moscow now invest regular hours in educational institutions of all sorts, from public schools to scholarly institutes. The demand for educational help from other nations now exceeds the current supply. The former Soviet Union has literally flung open its doors, issuing a Macedonian call to the West for our help.

A large portion of this expatriate help comes from Christian organizations like Inter-Varsity, Navigators, and Campus Crusade for Christ, and each in their own way makes important contributions. One group at my university was prohibited from ministering here only a few years ago, but today its weekly meetings are advertised across the campus and draw about 100 university students. It's hard to believe, but the East-West Christian Organization Directory and Database Project has documented over 800 Western Christian organizations now working in Eastern Europe and the former Soviet Union (see Appendix C).

Just as exciting as the opportunities for direct Christian ministry are the opportunities that now exist in almost every field of education and learning, at almost every level. In the area of law, for example, the Christian Legal Society has sponsored conferences and seminars in Russia. In business, International Teams organizes seminars for Russians trying to increase their awareness and knowledge of the meaning and principles of market economics, cross-cultural communications, international business communications, customer service and management, and the difference that Christian principles and ethics can make. Teaching the English language is an especially open opportunity and now occurs in any number of settings. The field of medicine needs perhaps more help than any, to both meet current needs and retool the fifteen new countries for the future.

Educational exchanges for college students like that enjoyed by my dorm neighbors from the University of Pittsburg can influence an entire life and worldview. In the field of curriculum research, many former Soviet teachers, having discarded the official texts of the past, now beg for help in rewriting new courses of study. By one estimate Moscow needs 5,000 new secondary school teachers, and also funds for paper and printing new textbooks (many old Marxist textbooks are still used simply because funds are not available to replace them)—voids Westerners could help to fill. Russian Ministries, for example, is involved in a $300,000 project with a national curriculum institute to make available a Gospel of Mark with a commentary for every seventh grader in the Russian Republic. In the fall of 1991 a group of American evangelicals even had an audience with then-president Gorbachev, who assured them of how much he appreciated all the different forms of help from the West.

Alexander Solzhenitsyn once wrote that "school is the key to Russia's future! The task for weary parents and educators to bring up a fine young generation is both contradictory and complex. It cannot be achieved all at once, it takes endless effort. The entire system of public education must be rebuilt from scratch *with the finest forces rather than the refuse.*"[43] The editorialist who cited this quote went on to lament the lack of such "finest forces" to get the job done. He described the past Soviet system as a tragedy that had produced only conformists and cynics. Today in the former Soviet Union, as with many other social institutions, "the educational system has broken from its ideological moorings and must hunt for resources in the ruins of a shattered economy."[44] People in the West who want to do more than watch CNN reports of the tragedy here and wring their hands now have unprecedented opportunities to make a constructive difference in Russia and the former republics. Russia has extended an invitation, and now awaits responses to its RSVP. It invites us to invest in the lives of emerging leaders of the CIS.

43. Cited in an issue of *MN* (no further information).
44. Victoria Pope, "Marks and Lenin," *US News and World Report*, October 21, 1991, p. 50. Pope's article provides a short but interesting look at changes in the former Soviet educational system.

Conclusion

The party is over for Soviet communists, at least for now, but they remain in the wings, organized into only slightly redefined parties and waiting for any opportunity that the failure of democracy might present to them. Democracy, on the other hand, incubated for six years in the womb of Gorbachev's glasnost and perestroika, has now been born, but in its neonatal condition it still struggles for life, growth, health, and maturity. The political challenges for democracy remain enormous, and confront virtually every one of the former republics.

In Estonia, after a shaky twenty-two-month rule, Prime Minister Edgar Savisaar resigned amidst economic chaos and a no confidence vote in January 1992. In Georgia the mercurial Zviad Gamsakgurdia, who won 87 percent of the vote in the country's first free election, fights to be reinstated after a coup toppled his totalitarian regime and native son Eduard Shevardnadze returned to head a new Georgian State Council. Gamsakhurdia remains exiled in the Checheno-Ingush, a separatist region of southern Russia. Tensions continue to mount between Russia and the Ukraine over the Black Sea Fleet, economic relations, and even a territorial dispute that dates back to 1954. In the Central Asian region, the republic of Nagorno-Karabakh voted for independence in December 1991, but Azerbaijan attempts to finalize its four-year struggle to regain the land by annihilating 180,000 Armenians living there. In oil-rich Kazakhstan, the second largest republic next to Russia, President Nursultan Nazarbayev embodies the contradictions of the new "democratic autocrat." Food riots by students in Uzbekistan have already killed several people. The Muslim world, both secular like Turkey and theocratic like Iran, now competes to influence the former Muslim republics that stretch across the Islamic crescent from Azerbaijan to Kirghiz, and include Uzbekistan, Tajikistan, and Turkmenistan—a total of some 50 million people. The Islamic Renaissance party, founded in 1990, has the goal of Islamic revolution, and now has chapters in Russia, Tajikistan, and Uzbekistan.[45] At the time of this

45. See "Five New Nations Ask, 'Who Are We?'" a short article on the six Muslim republics in Central Asia, featured in *Time*, April 27, 1992, pp. 44–46.

writing Tajikistan president Rakhmon Nabiyev was being ousted by Islamic opposition forces. In Moldavia, clashes continue in the break-away Trans-Dniestria region between Slav separatists who want to secede from the republic, and the government forces, who are primarily Romanian in their ethnic background. Moldavian president Mircea Snegur has declared a state of emergency. In the Russian Republic itself, the linchpin of democracy's fortunes, two regions have declared independence, both primarily Muslim in makeup—Chechen and Tartarstan. Boris Yeltsin still struggles to prove himself as a leader on the world stage of superpower politics.

Still, gains made by glasnost, the spirit of democracy, nuclear disarmament, and the world of education, all give cause for cautious optimism. As in the economic sphere, consolidating and advancing these gains will require help from the rest of the world, help that does not dominate but cooperates, does what is right rather than what is politically expedient, and creates responsible self-sufficiency rather than dependence. While failure could strike quickly, ultimate success will take a minimum of decades. But the time and the cost are worth it. In the interim, the fortunes of democracy in these fifteen new nations hang in the balance.

5

On Icons and Onion Domes: Christianity

By the authority conferred upon us by God we forbid you to approach the Holy Sacraments, and if you still call yourself Christians we anathematize you. . . . As for you, faithful sons of the church, we call upon you to stand in defense of our Holy Mother, now outraged and oppressed, . . . and should it become necessary to suffer for the cause of Christ, we call upon you to follow us on the way of suffering. . . . And you my brother bishops and priests. . . . without delay organize religious associations, call upon them to range themselves among the spiritual combatants who will resist physical force with the power of the Spirit. We firmly believe the enemies of the Church of Christ will be broken and scattered by the power of the cross, for the promise of Him who bore the cross is unalterable: "I will build my church and the gates of hell shall not prevail against it" (Matthew 16:18).

—Patriarch Tikhon (1866–1925)
Letter of February 1, 1918,
excommunicating the Bolsheviks

Introduction

As with so many other aspects of its life and history, the story of
Christianity in the former Soviet Union and the relationship between
throne and altar present the observer with ironies and paradoxes.
Westerners prone to view the country only as an evil empire of atheism need to review their history, for in fact, while the United States
was founded on the ideals of the Enlightenment as much as on anything else and is just now growing into historical adolescence at 200
years old, Russia treasures a millennium of a specifically Christian
heritage. Even after seventy years of virulent atheism it is estimated
that a greater percentage of the population in Russia attends church
(about 10 percent) than in nations in Western Europe. By 1914,
just before the Revolution, Russia was home to more than 1,000
monasteries.[1]

A Christian Heritage

Russia's Christian heritage began in Kiev. The story is told in the
Russian Primary Chronicle, the earliest historical record of Kiev, of
how Prince Vladimir of Kiev determined to find the true religion
by sending out a team of ambassadors to examine the world's religions. The delegation first encountered Bulgar Muslims of the Volga,
but considered them uncouth and hysterical: "there is no joy among
them but mournfulness and a great smell; and there is nothing good
about their system," they told Vladimir. In Germany and Rome they
"beheld no beauty" among Western Christians; but at Constantinople (present-day Istanbul) they attended the Divine Liturgy of
Saint John Chrysostom (the normal liturgy for Sundays and week-
days) in the Church of the Holy Wisdom and were awestruck at the
magnificent beauty and glory of Eastern Christianity. According to
the chronicler, it was as if heaven had invaded earth:

> The Greeks led us to the building where they worship their God,
> and we knew not whether we were in heaven or on earth. For on
> earth there is no such splendor or beauty, and we are at a loss to
> describe it. We know only that God dwells there among men, and

1. Timothy Ware, *The Orthodox Church* (New York: Penguin Books, 1964), p. 130.

their service is fairer than the ceremonies of other nations. For we cannot forget that beauty. Every man, after tasting something sweet, is afterward unwilling to accept that which is bitter.[2]

Subsequently, in 988 Prince Vladimir was baptized as a Christian, and 1,000 years later, in 1988, Russians celebrated a millennium of Christianity. The Orthodox love to recall this story, and I was interested when one evening over dinner in my apartment a Russian psychiatrist friend recounted this very story from *The Russian Primary Chronicle* in telling about her own conversion. Like the emissaries of Vladimir, she was drawn to Christianity by the beauty of the Orthodox liturgy.

Vladimir led the nation in a zealous and unquestioning embrace of Eastern Christianity that outdid even Byzantium. Mass baptisms took place; cathedrals were built; priests, relics, sacred vessels, and liturgies were imported; monasteries flourished; the pagan idol of the god Perun was toppled; church courts were started; and tithes were instituted. When he rejected paganism to adopt Christianity, and by-passed Western Christianity in favor of what has become known as Eastern Orthodoxy, Prince Vladimir "determined the destiny of Russia. . . . The whole Russian mind and heart were shaped by this eastern Christian mold."[3] In its wake, Vladimir's baptism spawned not merely a faith for private individuals, but "a whole Christian culture and civilization."[4] A student of mine, Natasha, once remarked that the Orthodox Church in Russia "is something far more than simply church; it's an entire culture."

Like Kiev, Moscow was founded not merely as a political or economic entity but as an explicitly Christian civilization that had a sense of a "manifest destiny" even greater than that exhibited by the founders of the United States. One scholar refers to this self-conscious sense of Christian destiny as a "Muscovite messianism" whereby Russians confidently saw themselves as God's elect people. At the time of its rise to greatness in the twelfth century, Moscow was something of a "revivalist camp"; by the sixteenth century and

2 Cited in Billington, *Icon and the Axe,* pp. 6–7.
3. Fedotov, *Russian Religious Mind,* p. 21.
4. Ware, *Orthodox Church,* p. 86.

the reign of Ivan the Terrible (1533–84) a "radical monasticization of society" had virtually eliminated secular culture: "By the time of Ivan the Terrible, Muscovy had set itself off even from other Orthodox Slavs by the totality of its historical pretensions and the religious character of its entire culture."[5] Today visitors to Moscow can still enjoy the treasures of this Christian legacy, for example, within the walls of the Kremlin itself, where at Cathedral Square a half-dozen magnificent churches dating back to the fifteenth century (and icons dating to the eleventh century) stand adjacent to the Palace of Congresses, the seat of government of the atheistic Soviet Union. They silently witness to a 1,000-year Christian heritage.

Westerners might be shocked to learn that for some, Moscow was precisely the opposite of a center of an atheistic, evil empire; it was known as the "third Rome." After his conversion, Emperor Constantine moved the capital of the Roman Empire from Rome to Constantinople, where for the next 1,100 years it served as the center of Eastern Christendom. At the second ecumenical council of Constantinople in 381, this new center of the empire was acknowledged as "the New Rome" (Canon 111), an honor reaffirmed by the Council of Chalcedon in 451 (Canon 28), which acknowledged Constantinople as second in prestige only to Rome. But when the Turks sacked Constantinople in 1453, Moscow fell heir to the title as the new protectorate of Christian civilization.

Historians trace the origin of this idea of Moscow as the "third Rome" to the monk Philotheus of the Eleazer Monastery in Pskov, who in 1510 wrote a letter to Tsar Basil III; in it he heralded Moscow as the third Rome:

> The church of ancient Rome fell because of the Apollinarian heresy; as to the second Rome—the Church of Constantinople—it has been hewn by the axes of the Hagarenes. But this third, new Rome, the Universal Apostolic Church under thy mighty rule, radiates forth the Orthodox Christian faith to the ends of the earth more brightly than the sun. . . . In all the universe thou art the only Tsar of Christians. . . . Hear me, pious Tsar, all Christian kingdoms have con-

5. Billington, *Icon and the Axe,* pp. 61, 69.

verged in thine alone. Two Romes have fallen, a third stands, a fourth
there shall not be.[6]

Ivan III's ("The Great") marriage to Sophia in 1472, the niece of
the last Byzantine emperor, also helped to establish Moscow as the
successor to Constantinople. Like Kiev, Moscow has been home to
ancient and long-standing Christian traditions.

Challenges to This Heritage

But this is only one part of Russia's religious history. More violent
cross-currents have muddied the river of Russian Christianity. Secular forces, some of its own making, have challenged Christianity for
centuries. Mongol pagans of Genghis Khan sacked Kiev in 1237
and ruled until 1480. The fall of Constantinople to the Turks in
1453 thrust Moscow into the position of the leader of Eastern Christendom, but it also severed Russian Christians from their spiritual
forebears of the south. Under Peter the Great (1689–1725), whom
Old Believer Orthodox Christians considered the Anti-Christ, the
patriarchate was abolished and replaced with the "Holy Synod,"
which in fact was an arm of the state government. Its members were
nominated by the emperor and it ruled the church until 1917. For
Peter and his program of Western secularization, the church was a
backward-looking, nationalistic, and bothersome impediment to
reform that had to be subjugated in the name of "progress." His
Spiritual Regulations (1721) not only abolished the patriarchate; it
effectively abolished the vibrancy of church life. Priests were obliged
to spy on their parishoners, for example, and were prohibited from
leaving their parishes without special permission. Existing monasteries were closely monitored, and new ones could not be started
without permission from the state. Things fared little better for the
church in the post-Petrine period. Queens Elizabeth (1741–62) and
Catherine II the Great (1762–96) closed over half of the country's
monasteries and restricted the activities of those that remained
opened. Although the church always had its true saints during this

6. Ibid., p. 58; Ware, *Orthodox Church*, p. 113.

"Synodical Period," its integrity was greatly compromised by secularization and obsequiousness toward the state.

On November 5, 1917, the Russian Orthodox bishops finally threw off the shackles of the synodical government and restored the patriarchate. It heralded a new day, but alas one much different than they expected, for by that time an ominous new foe had appeared. Two weeks before the new Patriarch Tikhon was elected from among three nominees, Lenin and the Bolsheviks had taken control of St. Petersburg; only two days before Tikhon's election they overpowered Moscow. Orthodox Christians now faced a new foe, this one a Western heresy: radical Marxist atheism.

It is a sad irony that one of the greatest Christian nations became one of the most powerful purveyors of "scientific atheism." It is even sadder that it has become fashionable in the West, even among some Christian theologians, to invoke the legacy of Marx indiscriminately for the cause of the gospel. In fairness, liberation theology has toned down its unbridled enthusiasm for Marxism in the past decade, and Marx did have some helpful insights about socioeconomic issues. But in the final analysis, atheism is an inseparable element of Marxist-Leninism, and because of that it is ultimately inimical to the gospel. Three generations have been lost to this political religion, and as many as 50 million people killed for its cause.

Marx's virulent hostility toward religion is indisputable. In one of his most famous and radical expressions of the abolition of religion as fundamental to human liberation and self-sufficiency, an 1844 essay entitled *A Contribution to the Critique of Hegel's Philosophy of Right: Introduction,* Marx announced that

> the criticism of religion is the premise of all criticism. . . . Religious suffering is at the same time an expression of real suffering and a protest against real suffering. Religion is the sigh of the oppressed creature, the sentiment of a heartless world, and the soul of soulless conditions. It is the opium of the people. The abolition of religion as the *illusory* happiness of men, is a demand for their *real* happiness. . . . [W]hat proves beyond doubt the radicalism of German theory, and thus its practical energy, is that it begins from the resolute positive abolition of religion. The criticism of religion ends with the doctrine that *man is the supreme being for man,* that is, with the categorical

imperative to overthrow all circumstances in which man is humili-
ated, enslaved, abandoned, and despised.[7]

Whether one can be a socialist and a Christian is an interesting question open to discussion, but whether one can be an orthodox Marxist and at the same time a Christian is self-evident. The Marxist
worldview, when adopted by Soviet Russia, has had catastrophic
results for society in general and the church in particular. The conflict
between the two worldviews, Christian and atheistic, was inevitable,
for the Communist party sought not only to transform society, the
economy, and politics; it sought to create "a new kind of human
being, a 'new man.' It sought spiritual power."[8]

For Marx the abolition of religion was essential for a new individual self-consciousness. For Lenin atheism was necessary for social
revolution. Taking a Machiavellian tact whereby the ruler says one
thing but does the opposite, Lenin publically supported religious
freedom, but in practice his personal agenda was quite the opposite. Berdyaev described Lenin as "a passionate and convinced atheist and hater of religion." Although the communist campaign against
religion was more of an emotional tirade against so-called counterrevolutionaries rather than an erudite critique, what we have here,
according to Berdyaev, is "a complete methodology . . . for the fight
against religion. Anti-religious propaganda is imposed as a binding
duty upon all Soviet philosophers who are regarded as orthodox."[9]

In the early years of Lenin's Soviet state, in the realm of education,
for example, we learn that "a Soviet teacher must be guided by the
principle of the Party spirit of science; he is obliged not only to be an
unbeliever himself, but also to be an active propagandist of God-
lessness among others, to be the bearer of the ideas of militant pro-
letarian atheism. Skillfully and calmly, tactfully and persistently, the
Soviet teacher must expose and overcome religious prejudices in the

7. Cited in Robert Tucker, ed., *The Marx-Engels Reader*, 2d ed. (New York: Norton,
1978), pp. 54, 60.

8. Heller and Nekrich, *Utopia*, p. 136.

9. Nicholas Berdyaev, *The Origin of Russian Communism* (Ann Arbor: University of
Michigan Press, 1991), pp. 160, 164. For an excellent treatment of Lenin and religion, see
Bohdan Bociurkiw, "Lenin and Religion," in *Lenin: The Man, The Theorist, The Leader*, ed.
Leonard Shapiro and Peter Reddaway (New York: Frederick Praeger, 1967), pp. 107–34.

course of his activity in school and outside school, day in and day out."[10] The *Soviet Small Encyclopedia* (1920) put it this way: "in the Soviet Union for the first time in history, schools take up the task of combatting religion. The school became an antireligious institution." The campaign was "successful" too; under Lenin's direct orders, in 1922 alone 8,100 priests, nuns, and monks were executed.[11]

Following Lenin's death in January 1924, Stalin continued the war against religion. *Izvestia*, a government newspaper, noted that "religious ideology is one of the chief obstacles in the path of the socialist reconstruction of the country."[12] The year 1925 saw the formation of the "League of Militant Atheists," which published the monthly magazine *The Godless* for mass distribution. By the end of the decade Stalin launched a new offensive against the church with the amendment of Article 13 of the Soviet constitution that made propagation of religion a crime against the state. In 1932 an "antireligious five-year campaign" was announced, so that "by the first of May 1937 not a single house of prayer will be needed any longer in any territory of the Soviet Union, and the very notion of God will be expunged as a survival of the Middle Ages and an instrument for holding down the working masses."[13]

Stalin wrote that "the Party cannot be neutral toward religion. It conducts an anti-religious struggle against all and any religious prejudices because it stands for science, while religious prejudice runs counter to science. . . . Antireligious propaganda is the means by which the complete liquidation of the reactionary clergy must be brought about."[14] He made good on his word, too, undertaking an vehement campaign to annihilate the church. Because of his militant hostility to religion, unspeakable horrors were unleashed upon the

10. F. N. Oleschuk, *Uchitelskaya Gazeta* (November 26, 1949). Cited by Ware, *Orthodox Church,* p. 153.

11. Heller and Nekrich, *Utopia,* p. 137.

12. *Izvestia,* April 24, 1924. Cited by Walter Sawatsky, *Soviet Evangelicals Since World War II* (Scottdale, Pa.: Herald, 1981), p. 28.

13. See Heller and Nekrich, *Utopia,* pp. 265, 739.

14. Albert L. Weeks, ed., *Brassey's Soviet and Communist Quotations* (Washington: Pergamon-Brassey's International Defense Publishers, 1987), pp. 221–22. Cited by Kent R. Hill, *The Soviet Union on the Brink: An Inside Look at Christianity and Glasnost* (Portland: Multnomah, 1991), p. 61.

church and society. Tens of millions were killed. Millions more were exiled or imprisoned. "Of the 50,000 priests and 163 bishops before the revolution, only slightly more than 100 priests and 7 bishops remained at the outbreak of war [World War II]. One thousand monasteries and sixty seminaries had been closed."[15] By 1933 all but 100 of Moscow's 600 churches were closed; by 1941 98 percent of all Orthodox churches were closed.[16] Before the Revolution of 1917, some 50,000 Russian Orthodox churches existed, but by 1985 that number had dwindled to 7,000.[17] Thus it is that one anonymous bishop of the "catacomb" church declared that when the Bolsheviks took power and declared their intentions to liquidate the church, it was "probably, the only honest act in their entire political activity, for, because of the contradictions that separate them, there can be no agreement between these two camps."[18] Beyond the tragedy of millions of lost lives and thousands of closed churches, which historians like Robert Conquest and Roy Medvedev have documented, those now living in the former Soviet Union can testify anecdotally to the multifaceted dimensions of terror this atheistic outlook has inflicted upon 300 million people and their society.

Religious life under Khrushchev looked like it might offer some reprieve from the persecution; after all, in his secret speech in 1956 he exposed the horrible crimes of Stalin, and public proclamations were made to overcome the "personality cult" of the former president. Nevertheless, in 1958 a massive antireligious campaign was unleashed. From 1959 to 1961 the number of Orthodox churches fell from 20,000 to 7,000. Islam, too, was targeted; in 1959 there were 1,200 mosques in the USSR, but by 1971 that number had fallen to 300.[19]

15. Heller and Nekrich, *Utopia*, p. 407.

16. See Hill, *Soviet Union*, p. 84. On the Russian church under Marxist–Leninism, see Dmitry Pospielovsky, *The Russian Church under the Soviet Regime, 1917–1982*, 2 vol. (Crestwood, N.Y.: St. Vladimir's Seminary Press, 1984), especially Chapter 5, "The Holocaust of the 1930s," where he cites these same figures and more besides.

17. Elisabeth Rubinfien, "Orthodox Revival," *WSJE*, December 11, 1991, p. 7.

18. Pospielovsky, *Russian Church*, 1:163.

19. Heller and Nekrich, *Utopia*, pp. 673–77. Cf. also Sawatsky, *Soviet Evangelicals*, Chapter 5, "The Khrushchev Campaign Against Religion," pp. 131–56.

New Opportunities

Russian history has taken yet another ironic turn, and despite the massive efforts to exterminate religion (it was supposed to "wither away" according to Marx), the church survived. At midnight on Saturday April 25, 1992, for the first time since the 1917 Bolshevik Revolution—74 long years—Easter bells rang out from the Kremlin's Ivan the Great Bell-Tower, and indeed all across Moscow. "We lived through a nightmare," said Valentina Kondrativa, who was attending the Easter worship service. Svetlana Ryashkina had brought her two young sons: "I came to the services today because I want my children to have something to believe in. I like how older people are able to tell us about ancient culture and traditions. We don't know anything."[20] At long last the relentless Marxist criticism of religion has itself been criticized and found wanting. The nation that celebrated 1,000 years of Christianity and endured seven decades of militant atheism now has new and untold opportunities to return to and recover its spiritual heritage. Already on the horizon there are signs of genuine resurgence and revival. Examples of this new turn of history abound.

On October 9, 1990, the Soviet government passed "The Law on Freedom of Conscience," which formally signaled the end of the nation's creed of atheism. Whether the government insures in reality what it has passed on paper remains to be seen, but Christians around the world can only marvel and rejoice at the content of the new legislation.[21] The "Law on Freedom of Conscience" guarantees that citizens can confess and practice their religion without hindrance from the state, and that they can "express and spread [their] convictions." "No compulsion of any kind is permitted when a citizen decides his [or her] own attitude toward religion." In one of the most shocking provisions, Article 5 prohibits the state from financing atheism: "The state does not fund religious organizations or activity associated with the propaganda of atheism." Access to the highest levels of education is promised all citizens, regardless of their religious preferences. Religious groups are allowed to own

20. Wendy Sloane, "Kremlin Bells Peal for Easter," *MT*, April 28, 1992, p. 3.
21. For the complete text of the Law on Freedom of Conscience, see Hill, *Soviet Union*, pp. 475–85.

property, export and import religious literature, and worship without restrictions.

Encouraging evidence points to a new climate of openness. As mentioned in the previous chapter, over 1,000 Christian organizations from around the world now minister and evangelize in the former Soviet Union (see Appendix C). Campus Crusade for Christ reports that over 73 million people have seen the *Jesus Film* in Eastern Europe and the former Soviet Union. In 1991, nearly 5,000 Christian leaders from across the former Soviet Union attended the Billy Graham School of Evangelism. Evangelical professors now teach in major universities as visiting professors in faculties of philosophy, history, sociology, and the like. From my own organization (International Institute for Christian Studies), for example, professors have lectured at state universities in Moscow, Kiev, Kharkov, Nizhni-Novgorod, Yaroslavl, Novosibirsk, Rostov-on-Don, Alma-Ata, Tashkent, Azerbaijan, Riga, and St. Petersburg. Other organizations like Christian College Coalition and the Christian Legal Society have made significant contributions in just as many places. Even so, Soviet educators continue to implore Western Christians to assist them in countless ways, as in helping them retool their curriculums to include a moral foundation for their students. Russian sociologist Mikhail Matskovsky of Moscow's International Center for Human Values has studied the effect of the Ten Commandments on the society, acknowledging the necessity of a moral basis for society.

Alexander Yakovlev, a close advisor to former President Gorbachev, once observed that the problem of Russia was not just empty shelves but empty souls. With its 1,000-year history of Christianity, interrupted by seven decades of militant atheism, contemporary Russia offers Christians around the world a special challenge, a Macedonian call for help. But if we are to respond to that call for help in the most constructive way possible, we must proceed not only with humility, but with historical sensitivity to and appreciation for the complex religious heritage of the nation. With its checkered history, Russia will be a land of unique promise and potential for the kingdom of God. Despite the many new gains, problems remain: the challenge of religious pluralism (50 million Muslims in central Asia), political fragmentation, economic disintegration, and ethnic strife. Rather than aggravating these problems, the gospel of the Prince of Peace must prove itself as a way of conciliation and accord. Two ways Western Christians can foster kingdom growth in the former Soviet Union are to understand the role of the Russian Orthodox Church, and to assume the posture of a learner rather than a teacher. When we come to see ourselves as spiritual debtors, not only creditors, we assume a posture that facilitates kingdom growth for everyone concerned.

The Orthodox Church

Yeltsin's Inauguration

When Boris Yeltsin was inaugurated in July 1991 as the first ever popularly elected president of Russia, dignitaries of various religions were honored to sit in the front row at the regal ceremony in the magnificent Palace of Congresses at the Kremlin. But only one religious representative took the stage: Patriarch Aleksy II of the Russian Orthodox Church. In the words of the age-old litany, "to be Russian is to be Orthodox."

The Russian Orthodox Church is hardly the only Christian church or religious body in the former Soviet Union. Not only Baptists, Pentecostals, and Catholics, but Jews, Jehovah's Witnesses, Mormons, Moonies, Muslims, and other groups populate the religious landscape. But in terms of size and historical importance, the Orthodox Church overshadows all other groups combined. As Fedotov observed, Prince Vladimir's decision to follow the path of Eastern Christianity shaped the very mind and heart of the Russian nation. With a 1,000-year history and about 50 million adherents, by far the largest Christian group in the former Soviet Union, and the largest Orthodox body in the world, no Christian group in Russia even comes close in terms of size or historical influence.[22] Catholics, for example, are the next largest Christian group, but both the Ukrainian (Uniate) and Roman Catholic Churches are highly regionalized, the former in the Ukraine, the latter primarily in Lithuania. Each of these churches numbers only about 4 million adherents, a mere tenth the size of Russian Orthodoxy. To know Russia, one must know its Orthodox Church.

22. On Russian "evangelicals," see Sawatsky, *Soviet Evangelicals.*

The so-called Orthodox Church is actually not one church but a family of fifteen autocephalous or independent, self-governing churches. The fifteen churches are administratively separate but united in sacraments, discipline, and doctrine. "Eastern Orthodoxy" is thus a popular, generic term that refers to this collection of autonomous church bodies. As independent churches, these churches are not bound together by any centralized organization or person as with the papacy in Roman Catholicism, but within each Orthodox church there is a head, variously referred to as the patriarch, archbishop, or metropolitan. The following list includes the fifteen autocephalous Orthodox churches, with rough estimates of their size—but these are only estimates.[23] Distinctions must be made between adherents and true believers, conditions before, during, and after atheistic repression, and the like. Although small in size, the first four patriarchates are usually accorded special honor due to their unique histories:

Constantinople	3,000,000
Alexandria	250,000
Antioch	450,000
Jerusalem	60,000
Russia	50–75,000,000
Romania	18,000,000
Greece	9,000,000
Serbia	8,000,000
Bulgaria	6,000,000
Georgia	2,000,000
Cyprus	500,000
Poland	850,000
Albania	160,000
Czechoslovakia	150,000
Sinai	(less than 100)

Small bodies of the Orthodox exist in Finland, Japan, and China, although they are not autocephalous, and the Orthodox Church in America of over one million adherents has not yet gained its

23. See Ware, *Orthodox Church,* pp. 13–14.

independence from other Orthodox bodies but exists under their jurisdiction.

The World of Orthodoxy

In many ways and for many reasons the Orthodox Church is very different from Christian churches in the West, both Protestant and Catholic. Alexis Khomiakov, a nineteenth-century Orthodox lay theologian, advised that Western Christians were likely to find Orthodoxy "a new and unknown world." The newcomer who enters an Orthodox church for the first time is likely to be astonished, even bewildered, for truly the world of Orthodoxy is a world where, as Orthodox priest Timothy Ware put it, not only the answers but the questions themselves are different.

Above all the Orthodox Church is a liturgical church, a church of "smells and bells" as a friend of mine put it. One orthodox priest was once asked what, exactly, it was that the Orthodox believed. He responded that it would be better to ask not what they believed but how they worshiped. The newcomer to an Orthodox worship service will be struck with near sensory overload: the absence of any chairs or pews, the icons that in some churches cover nearly every inch of space on the walls, the smokey smell of incense, the sound of hundreds of crackling candles burning in memory of the dead, the ornate regalia of the priest's clothing (not to mention his traditional enormous beard), worshipers who prostrate themselves as they make the sign of the cross and kiss the icons, and the mysterious-sounding chanted, Slavonic liturgy that echoes throughout the high ceilings of the cathedral. This liturgical celebration is a matter of ultimate reverence for most worshipers, too. At one service in St. Petersburg I made the mistake of putting my hands in my pockets during the liturgy. An old *babushka* behind me ordered me to take them out. The newcomer to the world of Orthodoxy might even wonder whether this is even the same Christianity followed by Westerners!

A Truly Orthodox Tradition

The Orthodox churches have long prided themselves on being "the Church of the Seven Councils," so much so that in many ways the church is stuck in a backwards-looking, static posture that cannot see beyond the first eight centuries of the church. Those seven ecumenical councils recognized by the Orthodox Church are Nicea (325), Constantinople (381), Ephesus (431), Chalcedon (451), Constantinople II (553), Constantinople III (680), and Nicea II (787). Orthodoxy is justly proud of its deliberate attempt to maintain continuity with the apostolic tradition of this patristic past, a posture that John of Damascus neatly summarized when he wrote, "We do not change the everlasting boundaries which our fathers have set, but we keep the tradition, just as we received it."[24] Although its liturgical life may seem strange to the Western observer, and although some of its doctrinal distinctives are questionable, on almost all major issues of Christian theology Eastern Orthodoxy places itself squarely in the tradition of what Vincent of Lerins (c. 434) said was believed by Christians "everywhere, always and by all." "Unquestioning loyalty" to the patristic tradition remains a "continuing characteristic" of the Orthodox churches.[25]

The Schism of 1054

Despite efforts by Christians in the Greek East and Latin West to protect one of the essential marks of the true church, the unity of the body of Christ, toward the middle of the first millennium of Christianity political, cultural, economic, and theological factors joined together so that eventually the church suffered the so-called Great Schism in the year 1054. From that date forward the Eastern Orthodox churches have had their own, unique identity, separate from Protestants and Catholics. Other schisms had occurred and would occur in the Christian church (the Donatist Controversy in the fifth century, the schism in the Catholic Church from 1378 to 1417, the sixteenth-century Reformation), but the Great Schism of 1054 was the first one of such major consequence. Like a marital divorce, the schism was a process that developed across many years. The year 1054 simply identifies the denouement of a long and sad estrangement. On June 16 of that year Pope Leo IX dispatched his emissary, Cardinal Humbert, to the Church of the Holy Wisdom in Con-

---

24. John of Damascus, *On Icons* 2.12. Cited by Ware, *Orthodox Church,* p. 204.

25. Jaroslav Pelikan, *The Spirit of Eastern Christendom (600–1700)* (Chicago: University of Chicago Press, 1974), p. 9.

stantinople to deliver a Bull of Excommunication that anathematized Patriarch Michael Cerularius and Eastern Christians. The papacy charged "Greek heretics" with trying to "humiliate and crush the holy catholic and apostolic church," while Cerularius urged his followers to "flee the fellowship of those who have accepted the heretical Latins."[26]

Already by the fourth century the Eastern and Western empires were drifting apart. In the year 330 Emperor Constantine moved the capital of the Roman Empire from Rome to Constantinople (literally, "city of Constantine"). While the religious and political empire in the Byzantine East enjoyed stability for another 1,000 years, until the sack of Constantinople by Muslims in 1453, barbarian invasions of Rome in the late fifth century hastened the demise of Rome's political clout and prestige and severed the unity long enjoyed between citizens of the two empires. Language posed another practical problem. By the end of the sixth century neither group could speak the other's language: Few Greeks spoke Latin, and few Latins spoke Greek. The rise of Islam, beginning with Mohammed (died 632) was checked only at the Battle of Tours in 732 by Charles Martel, but by that time most of the eastern Mediterranean had fallen under Muslim control. While Christianity had once flourished in the Mediterranean region (Constantine had controlled the lands around the entire perimeter of the Mediterranean), its expansion was now forced to proceed north and south. That new geopolitical axis further severed Byzantine Christians and the capital at Constantinople from their Western counterparts. When Pope Leo III turned a deaf ear to objections from the Greek East and crowned Charlemagne emperor of the West on Christmas Day in the year 800, Byzantines refused to acknowledge Charlemagne's plea for recognition; they considered the formation of his Holy Roman Empire an act of political sabotage and the pope's complicity in the coronation an act of schism. For his part, Charlemagne's cultural renaissance was marked by strong anti-Greek sentiment, while in the theological realm he reproached the Greeks for failing to cite the proper form of the Nicene Creed that contained the *filioque* clause.

Beyond these political and cultural factors, a host of theological

26. Ibid., pp. 170–71.

matters rent the fabric of Christian unity in two. A number of general issues differentiated Christians in the East and West and added to their growing sense of mutual alienation. The Greeks allowed clergy to marry, while Catholics required celibacy. In the East local parish priests could administer the sacrament of confirmation while in the West only the bishop could. In celebrating the Eucharist Latins mixed the water with wine; Byzantine Christians did not. The West used unleavened bread while the east used leavened bread. Greeks incorporated the use of icons, a practice the West rejected as questionable at best and idolatrous at worst. Other differences of clerical beards and tonsure, fasting, and a different theological outlook altogether (Greeks were more speculative, Latins more practical) contributed to deteriorating relations between the two bodies, but two key theological controversies were more important than all the others put together and drove the final wedge between Catholics and the Orthodox: the papacy and the *filioque* clause in the Nicene Creed.

One result of the barbarian invasions of Rome was that the papacy filled the power vacuum created by the hapless emperors and greatly increased its political clout. Eastern Christians, much more inclined to appeal to ecumenical councils rather than a single ecclesiastical ruler, resented and resisted this encroaching power of the papacy and the theological scaffolding created to justify it. The Orthodox were willing to acknowledge that the bishop of Rome had a distinct honor, but ultimately they insisted that he was only "first among equals." The so-called Schism of Photius in 867 brought the East-West disagreement about the papacy to a head.

In 858 Photius was appointed as Orthodoxy's new patriarch of Constantinople, replacing Saint Ignatius who had been exiled and later resigned his duties. Followers of Ignatius refused to acknowledge the resignation, and both Photius and the Ignatians appealed to Pope Nicholas I (858–67) for support. After some investigation of the matter and overturning the decision of his legates to support the legitimacy of Photius's appointment, Nicholas supported Ignatius and deposed Photius. From the Eastern perspective Nicholas's decision was yet another instance of the Western pope trying to extend his power, to use the pope's own words from a letter of 865, "over all the earth, that is over every church." Eastern Christians would hear nothing of it.

For his part, Photius branded the entire Western church as heretical for inserting the *filioque* clause into the Nicene Creed. Originally the Nicene Creed read that the Holy Spirit proceeded "from the Father," although a later interpolation by the Western Church (why, where, or by whom are not known), ratified at the Council of Toledo (589), added the phrase to indicate that the Spirit proceeded from the Father "and the Son" (literally, *filioque*). Charlemagne, we observed above, made the opposite charge, and upbraided Eastern Christians for failing to include the interpolation. To the Orthodox the *filioque* amendment was not only contrary to the explicit instructions of the past ecumenical councils, a usurpation of the inviolable wisdom of the church fathers; it was also theologically untrue and threatened the doctrine of the Trinity. Exacerbating the whole affair, in 1009 the Orthodox Patriarch Sergius refused to include the name of the Catholic pope (Sergius IV) on the official list of bishops acknowledged as orthodox, called the Diptychs, thus effectively ending communion between the two branches of Christendom.

The last act of this drama began when Cardinal Humbert placed Pope Leo IX's Bull of Excommunication on the altar in Constantinople as Patriarch Cerlarius prepared to celebrate the liturgy. It ended with a final, tragic scene that even today Eastern Christians have never forgotten. During the Fourth Crusade of 1204, Western Crusaders sacked Constantinople and ransacked the Church of the Holy Wisdom, an almost unimaginable act of desecration from the viewpoint of Eastern Christians. Any vestige of hope remaining after the Bull of 1054 that churches of the East and West would reunify were dashed with the pillage of 1204.

Despite honest efforts at reunification between Catholics and Orthodox in councils at Lyon (1274) and Florence (1438–39), to this day the two bodies remain estranged. In Russia today the Orthodox Church continues to exhibit historical tendencies of religious (and nationalistic) xenophobia. In late 1991, the Russian Orthodox patriarch refused an invitation for the Orthodox Church to participate at a synod of Catholic bishops from around Europe, and in March 1992 they chose to limit discussions with Catholics to the latter's expansions into Russia rather than to discuss the issues that divide the two communions. Tensions between Ukrainian Catholics and the Orthodox persist, the former insisting that churches on their territory belonged to them until 1946 when Stalin liquidated Catholics and gave their properties to the Russian Orthodox Church, and that the properties should therefore be returned. The latter denounces Catholic expansionism into the former Soviet Union. Patriarch Aleksy has urged Orthodox followers to rally against what they see as Catholic proselytism in Russia. Metropolitan Filaret, head of the Orthodox Church in the Ukraine, has even denounced the pope as "evil" in a televised speech. Whether the two communions can move beyond the 900-year schism to Christian unity seems questionable at this point in time.[27]

Learning to Listen: Eastern Lessons for Western Believers

The Fallibility of all Christians

Western Protestants inclined to look at these matters with an air of spiritual condescension or disgust might do well to remember that our own communities have theological and ethical skeletons that occasionally tumble out of the closet. From Luther's anti-Semitic remarks or Calvin's complicity in the death of Servetus and repressive regime in Geneva, to present-day crass worldliness, sectarian fundamentalism, blatant materialism, and televangelist fiascos, Protestants have enough business of their own to attend without hurling repraisals at other Christians. In his *Institutes of the Christian Religion* Calvin confessed that at times even the true Christian church "swarmed with many faults" and that we should not be guilty of an "immoderate severity" when judging it. Truly, all of us carry the treasure of the eternal gospel in very earthen, sometimes earthy, vessels.

Protestant Objections to Orthodoxy

Thus, without any pride, and conscious of our own doctrinal and ethical shortcomings, we must acknowledge that Protestants take exception with a number of theological beliefs held by the Orthodox

27. See Kent Hill, "The Orthodox Church and a Pluralistic Society," an expanded version of a paper given on November 19, 1991, at a conference on "Soviet Pluralism—Now Irreversible?" sponsored by the Institute for the Study of Conflict, Ideology and Policy at Boston University. Hill's article will be published in a book sponsored by this conference. Complete bibliographical information on Hill's article is available from the institute.

Church.[28] Despite their unhappy estrangement, in general Orthodoxy and Catholicism are much more similar to one another than Protestantism is to either of them, and thus Protestant discomfort with elements of Catholicism is in many instances extended to Orthodoxy. Orthodoxy considers the seven ecumenical councils to be infallible, and the church's dogmatic definitions and canon laws "inspired by God."[29] Eastern believers vow to submit to the teaching magisterium of the church, a posture that tends to discourage private initiative to interpret the Bible for one's self and to leave matters of doctrine up to the "experts." Western Christians would find Orthodoxy's large body of canon law, the hierarchical ecclesiastical system, and the veneration not only of icons but of relics to be all quite strange. The concept of salvation as deification or *theosis* would startle many Protestants (see John 17:21; 2 Pet. 1:4). The Orthodox view of the sacraments is quite close to that of Catholicism; they adhere to seven sacraments, and subscribe to baptismal regeneration. Their view of the Lord's Supper includes a belief in both transubstantiation (Christ is physically present in the bread and wine) and propitiatory sacrifice. Orthodox Christians pray to the saints and angels and for the dead (cf. 1 Cor. 15:29). They especially venerate Mary, whom they believe was free from actual sin and was taken directly to heaven after her death so that today her tomb is believed to be empty (Mary's "bodily assumption"). The Orthodox Church also vigorously maintains that it alone is the one true Church of Christ, and whether there can even be salvation outside of Orthodoxy remains a debated question among some of them.

Lessons for Western Christians

Doctrinal disagreements must not obscure the fact, so often lost among Protestants, Catholics, and the Orthodox, that the primary

28. For introductions to Orthodox theology, in addition to the works by Ware and Pelikan already cited, see Sergius Bulgakov, *The Orthodox Church* (Crestwood, New York: St. Vladimir's Seminary Press, 1988). Thomas Hopko, *The Orthodox Faith*, 4 vol. (Crestwood, New York: St. Vladimir's Seminary Press, 1984). Vladimir Lossky, *The Mystical Theology of the Eastern Church* (Crestwood, New York: St. Vladimir's Seminary Press, 1986); *Orthodox Theology: An Introduction* (New York: n.p., 1978). John Meyendorf, *The Orthodox Church*, 2d ed. (Crestwood, New York: St. Vladimir's Seminary Press, 1981).

29 Thomas Hopko, *The Orthodox Faith: Doctrine* (Crestwood, New York: SVSP, 1984), 1:20.

and fundamental theological issues we all agree on outweigh those that separate us (the Trinity, creation, sin, virgin birth, salvation in Jesus Christ alone, and the second coming). Further, these very real and sometimes significant differences must not keep Western Christians from the far more salutary and edifying task of learning some important lessons from Orthodox Christians, about whom many of us have remained ignorant. Taking the posture of a grateful debtor rather than a patronizing creditor, we in the West are glad to learn from those in the East and to deepen our own experience and understanding of our mutual Christian faith. This does not mean we deny or obscure the above-mentioned differences as unimportant or insignificant; it only means we have the grace and maturity to learn from others who can teach us. Because of its own unique pilgrimage and theological vision, the Orthodox Church can instruct Western Christians in some valuable lessons. Three areas in particular stand out: the role of suffering, the mystery of God, and the role of tradition.

Despite centuries of flourishing churches, for the past seventy-five years the Orthodox Church has experienced unimaginable suffering for its Christian faith.[30] Only in the past five years or so has the intense repression eased and the church been able to begin the task of renewal and rebuilding. Earlier in this chapter we observed the great lengths to which Stalin went to liquidate the Orthodox Church, and the large degree, at least by some measures, to which he was successful: Millions of parishoners were killed; thousands of priests were exiled or slaughtered; churches were closed and turned into museums of atheism; most monasteries were shut down or destroyed; and privileges of education, employment, and the like were denied believers. When overt persecution was not used, more subtle means such as control via registration were employed.

Not all Orthodox priests or believers fared equally well under persecution; some endured, others recanted, not a few became tools of the state, and others made various compromises—just as happened in the first two centuries of the church when persecutions were severe. Even Patriarch Tikhon stood boldly against Lenin and

---

30. We must remember that the experience of the Orthodox was not unique in this regard; all people in Russia, not just Christians, suffered terribly the last seven decades.

his troops who came to power just when he was elected, but later made more conciliatory statements toward the state (he had been imprisoned, and maybe even brainwashed). In fairness to those Orthodox who cooperated with the Soviet state, some considered it the only way to survive and continue to minister, even if in greatly compromised and restricted ways. In addition to people like Tikhon, Orthodox priests like Alexander Men and Dmitry Dudko paid high prices for their faithfulness to the gospel under intense persecution. To those tempted to sit in judgment on believers who succumbed under persecution, Dudko had a poignant reminder, written in response to those who criticized Orthodoxy's obsequious posture toward the Soviet regime:

> Who has fewer civil rights than the patriarch? They say he is surrounded by thousands of informers. He so much as sighs and it's heard in every government department. Everything he does against his conscience he does under pressure, and, of course, out of weakness, like any man. But you don't want to be compassionate. You sit in the judge's seat and pronounce sentence.[31]

Rather than sit in the seat of judgment, Western Christians, most of whom have never known anything of suffering for Christ, should rather learn from the Orthodox experience of persecution.

Throughout the pages of the New Testament, in the early church, and throughout the world today, many Christians have had to endure intense suffering for the cause of Jesus Christ. If we read the New Testament closely, suffering for Christ is a much more prevalent theme than we in the West have cared to notice. Jesus warned his apostles about suffering (Matt. 24:9). Luke records the fulfillment of that promise (Acts 5:41). Every epistle of Paul except one contains some mention of suffering, either of Paul or his readers. Only the brief epistle to Titus does not contain such a reference. (Titus was Paul's missionary companion who was discharged to Dalmatia to settle the churches there; surely he too knew apostolic persecution and suffering.) The books of Hebrews, James, especially Peter, Jude, and Revelation likewise all speak eloquently to the reality of suffering

---

31. Cited by Hill, *Soviet Union*, p. 110.

in the early church. Not until Emperor Constantine's conversion in 313 did persecution stop for the early Christians.

Just as suffering can produce character (Rom. 5:3–4), and the blood of the martyrs can be the seed of the church (Tertullian), conversely, Christian existence in a land of ease can lead to spiritual flabbiness. It can also foster an ill-advised triumphalistic attitude, a "theology of glory" (*theologia gloriae*) which seeks to know God only through his mighty displays of victory, power, miracle, and glory. Of course, God has revealed himself in mighty acts of power, and we can read about them in both the Old and New Testaments and even in reports of Christians from around the world today. But it was Martin Luther's great contribution to remind us of the biblical truth that despite his many mighty acts of miracle and triumph, God's ultimate act of self-revelation was through suffering on a cross, and that those who wish to know and follow the Suffering Servant must likewise take up their own cross and follow in his footsteps down the *via dolorosa*. A "theology of the cross" (*theologia crucis*) recognizes that God is primarily known not through triumphalistic miracles or overt and startling displays of his power, but through times of great suffering, testing, and human weakness (cf. 2 Cor. 12:7–10). More than most Christians in the West, Orthodox believers have known through experience the power of this truth.

This does not mean Christians masochistically seek suffering. We must always seek to end suffering. But it does mean we reject the unbiblical ideas that God keeps his people immune from suffering, that he removes every persecution and heals every sickness, that dreadful tests and trials will never come our way, or that the presence of prolonged suffering reveals a believer's lack of faith. On occasion these sufferings are simply the result of living in a fallen world, while at other times they are a direct result of our Christian identity. The sixteenth-century Reformers made a helpful distinction on this point between "security" and "certainty." Certainty seeks guarantees of immunity—something, of course, that God has not given. Security, on the other hand, depends not on guarantees of immunity but on the promise of God's presence. False guarantees of immunity almost always fail sooner or later; they can cause incredible disappointment and disillusionment. But as the apostle Paul wrote, we can rejoice in our sufferings because they produce hope, and hope in God never

disappoints, for God has given us the security of his very self through
the presence of the Holy Spirit. Karl Barth made a similar distinction
when he wrote of the "assurance of faith" that does not seek some
"unequivocal experience . . . a guarantee of the guarantee, so to
speak . . .", that is, seeking some experience that would go beyond
"the guarantee which is identical with God Himself."[32]

Because of their own experience of intense and prolonged persecution Orthodox Christians in Russia and Eastern Europe have had
more opportunities to learn this vital, even normative according to
the New Testament, truth of Christian discipleship; may we in the
West have the wisdom to learn from their experiences, rejecting our
triumphalistic attitudes and theologies of glory in favor of the more
biblical idea of knowing God through the way of the cross.

A second way Christians can learn from the Orthodox tradition is
in the area of how we do theology or think about God. This was
brought home to me by one of my graduate students at Moscow
State University. Vasily is not even a theist, so it stunned me when
one day in our seminar he criticized the Christian scholar C. S. Lewis
and his book *Mere Christianty* for being "too logical." For Vasily,
Lewis's entire apologetic enterprise was needlessly bogged down in
rationalistic quicksand. Wasn't rationalism a virtue to cultivate rather
than a vice to avoid?! How could anyone be "too logical"? Vasily's
remark hints at an important perspective contained in Orthodox
theology.

Following in the tradition of Descartes, much Western theology is
very cognitive and rationally oriented. In his *Meditations on First
Philosophy* Descartes refused to believe any truth that was not entirely
"true and distinct" or "very clear," giving rise to a philosophical
tradition known as Cartesian rationalism. When adopted by some
theologians, Descartes' posture has led to theology that is highly
committed to empirical proofs, deductive logic, and the rational
intelligibility of nearly every theological concept, a standard of truth
that is much closer to the Enlightenment than to the Bible. Orthodoxy and the Russian mindset, on the other hand, as Vasily inti-
mated, have a much greater inclination toward the positive value of
mystery. They place a great emphasis on what has been called

32. *Church Dogmatics* 1.1.12.

"apophatic" theology or "the way of negation" (*apophasis*, denial), a theological vision that Westerners should find a helpful corrective to Cartesian rationalism.

Apophatic theology begins with the biblical affirmation that no person has seen or can see God (John 1:18), that his ways are, in the words of Isaiah quoted by Paul, "unsearchable" and "unfathomable" (Rom. 11:33–36). So-called negative theology recalls that even the angels shielded their vision of God (Isa. 6:2), and that according to Isaiah and Paul there is a qualitative difference between human and divine wisdom (Isa. 55:8–9; 1 Cor. 1:18–31; 3:18–23). In short, God's being and ways are far above ours, and we need to be careful that in our theology we do not fashion him in our own image. This biblical emphasis came to occupy a large place in the theological vision of Orthodoxy.

Following the sixth-century thinker Dionysius the Pseudo-Areopagite, an anonymous writer once thought to be Paul's convert (Acts 17:34), Orthodoxy is mindful that God is beyond knowing, and that all we know about him is best expressed with negative qualifiers, saying what God is not (God is not finite, he does not change, and so on). Orthodoxy's great theologians have always emphasized this transcendent mystery of God, so much so that one theologian and priest, Timothy Ware, writes that "all true Orthodox theology is mystical."[33]. The Greek theologian John of Damascus (675–749) exemplifies this theological vision, writing,

> *that* there is a God is clear; but what He is by essence and nature, this is altogether beyond our comprehension and knowledge. . . . God is infinite and incomprehensible, and all that is comprehensible about Him is His infinity and incomprehensibility. . . . God does not belong to the class of existing things; not that he has no existence, but that he is above all existing things, nay, above existence itself.[34]

Maximus Confessor (580–662), another of Orthodoxy's greatest theologians, wrote that "a perfect mind is one which, by true faith,

---

33. Ware, *Orthodox Church*, p. 215.
34. John of Damascus, *The Orthodox Faith* 1.4. Cited by Ware, *Orthodox Church*, pp. 73, 217.

in supreme ignorance knows the supremely unknowable one,"[35] and that "the ignorance about God on the part of those who are wise in divine things is not a lack of learning, but a knowledge that knows by silence that God is unknown."[36] Knowledge of God is, therefore, a type of "learned ignorance." More broadly, in its liturgical life we see how the Orthodox love for sight, sound, and smell (icons, bells, and incense), over the spoken word, models and incarnates this apophatic emphasis on the mysterious and aesthetic over the cognitive and the rational.[37]

The apophatic theological vision is careful to avoid any sort of pious agnosticism or skepticism, and much more any irrational retreat into subjectivity as was evidenced in the fourteenth-century sectarian movement known as Hesychasm (*hesychia,* inner calm). Instead, it signals a theological modesty that appreciates the immensity of God and the fraility of human reason. Human knowledge about God is restricted by our finitude, our sinfulness, our earthbound condition, and our cultural blinders. But because we are created in the image of God, and because God has revealed himself in the mystery of the cross, people can know him through faith. Thus there is a balance to maintain, between hyper-rationalism on the one hand, and subjectivity on the other, hinted at by the writer of Ecclesiasticus 3:21–22: "Seek not what is too difficult for you, nor investigate what is beyond your power. Reflect upon what has been assigned to you, for you do not need what is hidden."[38] We can sumarize all of this by saying that Christians enjoy a limited but valid knowledge of God.

In his better moments Descartes confessed that there were many things about God that were "impenetrable" and "beyond the powers of my mind."[39] Positively stated, the most famous expression of this theological method is found in Anselm of Canterbury (1033–1109), who in his *Proslogion* wrote that "I do not seek to understand in

35. Maximus, *Four Centuries on Charity* 3.99.

36. Maximus, "*On the Divine Names" of Dionysis the Areopagite* 7.1. The two citations by Maximus are taken from Pelikan, *Spirit of Eastern Christendom,* pp. 33–34.

37. Cf. Billington, *Icon and the Axe,* pp. 33, 38. According to Billington, Orthodox thought tended to "crystallize in images rather than in ideas" (p. 35).

38. Cited by Pelikan, *Spirit of Eastern Christendom,* p. 31.

39. Descartes, *Meditations on First Philosophy,* trans. Laurence J. Lafleur (Indianapolis: Bobbs-Merrill, 1979), p. 53. Cf. pp. 57, 79.

order to believe, but I believe in order to understand. For this too, I believe, that 'unless I believe, I shall not understand.'"[40] In Orthodox theology, this impenetrable mystery of God is not something to lament or to expunge by some rationalistic demand to satisfy the canons of linear logic, but something to affirm and celebrate in reverent worship. In this area, too, Eastern Christians have enjoyed a biblical tradition that perhaps some Western believers would do well to recover.

Perhaps nothing typifies Orthodoxy so much as its self-conscious adherence to tradition, a determination to pattern its life and theology after the early church fathers and ecumenical creeds. Many analysts would identify this orientation to apostolic tradition as the characteristic mark of Orthodoxy, a hallmark that "pervades every aspect of Orthodox life."[41] The words of John of Damascus bear repeating, that "we do not change the everlasting boundaries which our fathers have set, but we keep the tradition, just as we received it."[42] Here too, despite an important disagreement with Protestantism, Western Christians can deepen their understanding of and commitment to the gospel.

The idea of adhering to the apostolic "tradition" is itself a New Testament one (*paradosis*). Although Christ refers to "human traditions" in a negative way (Mark 7:9), the apostles employed the word in a positive sense. Paul repeatedly speaks of having received and in turn passed on the apostolic tradition, and he constantly implores his listeners to preserve it (1 Cor. 11:2; 15:3; 2 Thess. 2:15). Luke assures his readers that he was very careful in the sources he used to pass on the Jesus tradition (Luke 4:1–4). Of course, for the decades prior to the writing of the New Testament, this tradition was an oral one.

For its part, Orthodoxy extends the idea of tradition to mean much more than written texts. "It is, on the contrary, the total life and experience of the entire Church transferred from place to place and from generation to generation. Tradition is the very life of the Church itself as it is inspired and guided by the Holy Spirit."[43] Pri-

---

40. Anselm, *Proslogion,* Chapter 1. The quotation is from Isa. 7:9.
41. Ware, *Orthodox Church,* p. 203.
42. John of Damascus, *On Icons* 2.12. Cited by ibid., p. 214.
43. Hopko, *Orthodox Faith,* 1:12.

mary sources of tradition would include the Bible and the first seven ecumenical councils, along with the patristic period of the "fathers," but it would also include in a secondary sense later councils, the church liturgy, canon law, and even icons.

Here, of course, Orthodoxy and Protestantism part company. Although in principle Orthodox theologians refer to the Bible as the "supreme" expression of tradition, or as having an honor of "first place," they extend the concept of infallibility even to the ecumenical councils and canon law. Protestants, on the other hand, following the enormous influence of Martin Luther, have insisted that councils "can and do err," and that Scripture alone (*sola Scriptura*) is the exclusive vehicle of God's self-revelation. Put another way, in Orthodoxy the Scriptures and the other forms of tradition are coequal, while in Protestantism Scripture alone is primary, *sui generis* ("of its own kind, or in a class by itself"), and other forms of tradition, while not antithetical to Scripture, are seen as qualitatively secondary to it. In Orthodoxy there is a continuity between the forms of tradition; in Protestantism there is a discontinuity between Scripture and the other types of tradition. This difference maintained by Protestants against Orthodoxy is not only very important, but also valid and necessary. In practice, however, there is more to this matter than meets the eye.

Protestants have always been the beneficiaries of tradition, even though they have been slow to understand or admit this, and they have even formed their own traditions (some good and some bad) which at times have been as inflexible and authoritarian as any found in Orthodoxy. Sadly and ironically, this blindness to our own tradition(s) has often been accompanied by an explicit antipathy toward tradition in favor of *sola Scriptura,* an antipathy that too often has thrown out the baby with the bath water. While rightly adhering to the primacy of Scripture, for several reasons Western Protestants need to recover a sense of the validity and importance of a broader role for tradition. The Orthodox perspective helps us in this necessary task.

What should a Protestant understanding of "tradition" include? We can follow the wisdom of Methodist theologian Thomas Oden, who like few others has advised this rejuvenation of tradition. Oden is fond of citing Lancelot Andrews, a sixteenth-century Anglican, to illustrate what he means by the central, apostolic tradition: "one canon, two testaments, three creeds (Apostles', Nicene, Athanasian), four ecumenical councils (Nicea, Constantinople, Ephesus, and Chalcedon), and five centuries along with the fathers of that period."[44] Elsewhere he has employed a geometric metaphor of a center with a wide circumference. The "vital center" of Christian tradition is found in Scripture as the "incomparable textual center of orthodoxy," supplemented by the three venerable creeds, the seven ecumenical councils, and the eight great theologians of the East (Athanasius, Basil, Gregory Nazianzus, Chrysostom) and West (Ambrose, Augustine, Jerome, and Gregory). The "wide circumference" extends up through the modern age to those who clearly follow in the footsteps of the aforementioned.[45] Protestants need to recover a sense of tradition, so defined, for a number of reasons.

Tradition is not merely helpful; in some instances it is necessary. In the fifth century the theologian Vincent of Lerins (d. c. 450) discovered this truth when he pondered an important problem: How could he determine what to believe as orthodox Christianity and what to reject as heresy? He noted that some people advised him to follow "Scripture alone," but Vincent responded that this was not entirely helpful because everyone, even the heretics, claimed to follow Scripture, and besides, Scripture can be interpreted in many different ways! Surely, thought Vincent, there must be some rule, some method, to distinguish between the standard of true Christianity and its perversions. In his *Commonitorium* (434) Vincent determined that it is necessary to turn to tradition. Christians must adhere to what has been believed "everywhere, always, by all." In other words, the threefold test of "universality, antiquity, and consent" helps us to distinguish true faith from its counterfeits.

In addition to helping us to distinguish the true from the false, a knowledge of the historical, apostolic tradition can help Protestants to distinguish between the important and the peripheral, between what is theologically essential and what is superfluous, between that

44. Thomas Oden, "Back to the Fathers," *Christianity Today*, September 24, 1990, p. 28.

45. Thomas Oden, "Then and Now: The Recovery of Patristic Wisdom," *The Christian Century*, December 12, 1990, p. 1167. For a longer exposition of Oden's particular theological method, see Daniel B. Clendenin, "Thomas Oden," in *Handbook of Evangelical Theologians*, ed. Walter Elwell (Grand Rapids: Baker, 1993).

which is non-negotiable in our faith and that which is open for discussion. In other words, a knowledge of the early Christian tradition found in the creeds and the apostolic fathers of the first centuries helps us to gain a sense of perspective or priority in doctrine, and to avoid majoring on minor points. By focusing on the essential core of the faith, Christians can avoid sectarian tendencies and free themselves to a broader usefulness in the kingdom of God. Paul himself hints at such a "hierarchy" of important doctrines when in 1 Corinthians 15:1–3 he passes on to the Corinthians the theological tradition of those things that were of "first importance."

Without any compromise of their distinction between Scripture and tradition, Protestants can learn from the Orthodox love of tradition. Following "tradition" is inevitable. The only question is whether our traditions will be like the human ones so vehemently scorned by Christ, or the essential ones repeatedly enjoined by the apostle Paul. Vincent of Lerins shows us that knowing the true apostolic tradition is not only inevitable but necessary. Further, loving the patristic past helps us to love what is essential and normative and to put peripheral doctrines in their proper place.

Conclusion

The paradigm of suffering for salvation. The majesty of mystery. The tapestry of apostolic tradition. Protestants need have no fear of compromising their own distinctives when they learn from the Orthodox Church about these three important areas of Christian life and doctrine. Taking the posture of a grateful learner, Christians of the West who learn from those in the East model the unity that our Lord said would characterize his people (John 17:20–23). They hasten the coming kingdom on earth, even as it is in heaven.

APPENDIX A

Resignation of President Mikhail S. Gorbachev

Dear fellow countrymen, compatriots. Due to the situation which has evolved as a result of the formation of the Commonwealth of Independent States, I hereby discontinue my activities at the post of President of the Union of Soviet Socialist Republics.

I am making this decision on considerations of principle. I firmly came out in favor of the independence of nations and sovereignty for the republics. At the same time, I support the preservation of the union state and the integrity of this country.

The developments took a different course. The policy prevailed of dismembering this country and disuniting the state, which is something I cannot subscribe to.

After the Alma-Ata meeting and its decisions, my position did not change as far as this issue is concerned. Besides, it is my conviction that decisions of this caliber should have been made on the basis of popular will.

However, I will do all I can to insure that the agreements that were signed there lead toward real concord in society and facilitate the exit out of this crisis and the process of reform.

Resignation speech of Mikhail S. Gorbachev, former president of the Union of Soviet Socialist Republics, presented on Russian television on December 25, 1991. Reprinted in Vital Speeches of the Day 58 (January 15, 1992): 194–96.

This being my last opportunity to address you as President of the U.S.S.R., I find it necessary to inform you of what I think of the road that has been trodden by us since 1985.

I find it important because there have been a lot of controversial, superficial, and unbiased judgments made on this score. Destiny so ruled that when I found myself at the helm of this state it already was clear that something was wrong in this country.

We had a lot of everything—land, oil and gas, other natural resources—and there was intellect and talent in abundance. However, we were living much worse than people in the industrialized countries were living and we were increasingly lagging behind them. The reason was obvious even then. This country was suffocating in the shackles of the bureaucratic command system. Doomed to cater to ideology, and suffer and carry the onerous burden of the arms race, it found itself at the breaking point.

All the half-hearted reforms—and there have been a lot of them— fell through, one after another. This country was going nowhere and we couldn't possibly live the way we did. We had to change everything radically.

It is for this reason that I have never had any regrets—never had any regrets—that I did not use the capacity of General Secretary just to reign in this country for several years. I would have considered it an irresponsible and immoral decision. I was also aware that to embark on reform of this caliber and in a society like ours was an extremely difficult and even risky undertaking. But even now, I am convinced that the democratic reform that we launched in the spring of 1985 was historically correct.

The process of renovating this country and bringing about drastic change in the international community has proven to be much more complicated than anyone could imagine. However, let us give its due to what has been done so far.

This society has acquired freedom. It has been freed politically and spiritually, and this is the most important achievement that we have yet fully come to grips with. And we haven't, because we haven't learned to use freedom yet.

However, an effort of historical importance has been carried out. The totalitarian system has been eliminated, which prevented this country from becoming a prosperous and well-to-do country a long time ago. A breakthrough has been effected on the road of democratic change.

Free elections have become a reality. Free press, freedom of worship, representative legislatures and a multi-party system have all become reality. Human rights are being treated as the supreme principle and top priority. Movement has been started toward a multi-tier economy and the equality of all forms of ownership is being established.

Within the framework of the land reform, peasantry began to reemerge as a class. And there arrived farmers, and billions of hectares of land are being given to urbanites and rural residents alike. The economic freedom of the producer has been made a law, and free enterprise, the emergence of joint stock companies and privatization are gaining momentum.

As the economy is being steered toward the market format, it is important to remember that the intention behind this reform is the well-being of man, and during this difficult period everything should be done to provide for social security, which particularly concerns old people and children.

We're now living in a new world. An end has been put to the cold war and to the arms race, as well as to the mad militarization of the country, which has crippled our economy, public attitudes and morals. The threat of nuclear war has been removed.

Once again, I would like to stress that during this transitional period, I did everything that needed to be done to insure that there was reliable control of nuclear weapons. We opened up ourselves to the rest of the world, abandoned the practices of interfering in others' internal affairs and using troops outside this country, and we were reciprocated with trust, solidarity, and respect.

We have become one of the key strongholds in terms of restructuring modern civilization on a peaceful democratic basis. The nations and peoples of this country have acquired the right to freely choose their format for self-determination. Their search for democratic reform of this multinational state had led us to the point where we were about to sign a new union treaty.

All this change had taken a lot of strain, and took place in the context of fierce struggle against the background of increasing resistance by the reactionary forces, both the party and state structures, and the economic elite, as well as our habits, ideological bias, the sponging attitudes.

The change ran up against our intolerance, a low level of political culture and fear of change. That is why we have wasted so much time. The old system fell apart even before the new system began to work. Crisis of society as a result aggravated even further.

I'm aware that there is popular resentment as a result of today's grave situation. I note that authority at all levels, and myself are being subject to harsh criticisms. I would like to stress once again, though, that the cardinal change in so vast a country, given its heritage, could not have been carried out without difficulties, shock and pain.

The August coup brought the overall crisis to the limit. The most dangerous thing about this crisis is the collapse of statehood. I am concerned about the fact that the people in this country are ceasing to become citizens of a great power and the consequences may be very difficult for all of us to deal with.

I consider it vitally important to preserve the democratic achievements which have been attained in the last few years. We have paid with all our history and tragic experience for these democratic achievements, and they are not to be abandoned, whatever the circumstances, and whatever the pretexts. Otherwise, all our hopes for the best will be buried. I am telling you all this honestly and straightforwardly because this is my moral duty.

I would like to express my gratitude to all people who have given their support to the policy of renovating this country and became involved in the democratic reform in this country. I am also thankful to the statements, politicians and public figures, as well as millions of ordinary people abroad who understood our intentions, gave their support and met us halfway. I thank them for their sincere cooperation with us.

I am very much concerned as I am leaving this post. However, I also have feelings of hope and faith in you, your wisdom and force of spirit. We are heirs of a great civilization and it now depends on all and everyone whether or not this civilization will make a comeback to a new and decent living today. I would like, from the bottom of my heart, to thank everyone who has stood by me throughout these years, working for the righteous and good cause.

Of course, there were mistakes made that could have been avoided, and many of the things that we did could have been done better. But I am positive that sooner or later, some day our common efforts will bear fruit and our nations will live in a prosperous, democratic society.

I wish everyone all the best.

President Bush Remarks on Mikhail S. Gorbachev's Resignation

By GEORGE BUSH, President of the United States of America
Televised to the Nation, Washington, D.C., December 25, 1991

Mikhail S. Gorbachev's resignation as President of the Soviet Union culminates a remarkable era in the history of his country and in its long and often difficult relationship with the United States. As he leaves office, I would like to express publicly, and on behalf of the American people, my gratitude to him for years of sustained commitment to world peace, and my personal respect for his intellect, vision and courage.

President Gorbachev is responsible for one of the most important developments of this century—the revolutionary transformation of a totalitarian dictatorship and the liberation of his people from its smothering embrace.

His personal commitment to democratic and economic reform through perestroika and glasnost—a commitment which demanded the highest degree of political and personal ingenuity and courage—permitted the peoples of Russia and other republics to cast aside decades of dark oppression and put in place the foundations of freedom.

Working with President Reagan, myself and other allied leaders, President Gorbachev acted boldly and decisively to end the bitter divisions of the Cold War and contributed to the remaking of a Europe whole and free.

His and Foreign Minister Eduard Shevardnadze's "new thinking" in foreign affairs permitted the United States and the Soviet Union to move from confrontation to partnership in the search for peace across the globe. Together we negotiated historic reductions in chemical, nuclear and conventional forces and reduced the risk of a nuclear conflict.

Working together, we helped the people of Eastern Europe win their liberty and the German people their goal of unity in peace and freedom. Our partnership led to unprecedented cooperation in repelling Iraqi aggression in Kuwait, in bringing peace to Nicaragua and Cambodia, and independence to Namibia. And our work continues as we seek a lasting and just peace between Israelis and Arabs in the Middle East, and an end to the conflict in Afghanistan.

President Gorbachev's participation in these historic events is his legacy to his country and to the world. This record assures him an honored place in history and, most importantly for the future, establishes a solid base from which the United States and the West can work in equally constructive ways with his successors.

APPENDIX B

Principal Political Parties and Public Movements of Russia, April 1992

1. The Anarcho-Syndicalist Conference (5-2-89).
2. The Anarcho-Democratic Conference (4-17-90).
3. The Anarcho-Communist Revolutionary Union (1989).
4. The Association of Anarchist Movements (6-16-90).
5. The Army in Defense of the Biosphere (n.d.).
6. The United Council of Russia Association—People's Accord (9-9-89).
7. The White Guard (n.d.).
8. The Vatan Organization (10-13-90).
9. Movement in Defense of Communists' Rights (12-19-91).
10. The Servicemen for Democracy Movement (10-13-91).
11. The Revival Party (10-26-91).
12. The Universe and Mankind's Salvation Movement (n.d.).
13. The All-Russia Russian Assembly (n.d.).
14. The All-Union Anti-Fascist Center (2-20-88).

This list is from Tass news agency's stenographic bulletins service. The original list, available from the author, contains brief annotations about each party—when they were founded, key leaders, size of membership, basic orientation, addresses, and telephone numbers. After the organization, in parentheses, is the date when the party was founded.

15. The All-Union Movement of Komsomol Supporters (11-7-91).
16. The All-Church Orthodox Youth Movement (11-91).
17. The Humanitarian Party (7-90).
18. The Civil Concord Party (10-90).
19. The Movement for Freedom and Democracy (7-89).
20. The Constructive Forces Movement (7-6-91).
21. The Assembly of Russian Noblemen—The Union of Descendants of Russian Noblemen (n.d.).
22. The Democratic Option Movement (10-90).
23. The Democratic Congress (1-26-91).
24. The Democratic Union (5-7-88).
25. The Democratic Moscow Forum (n.d.).
26. The Democratic Party (10-5-90).
27. The Democratic Party of Russia (n.d.).
28. The Democratic Party of the USSR (8-5-89).
29. The Democratic Workers' Party (Marxist) (3-24-90).
30. The Democratic Russia Bloc (1-26-91).
31. The Democratic Movement of Communists (11-17-90).
32. The Unity for Leninism and Communist Ideals Organisation—All-Union Communist Party of Bolsheviks (5-18-89).
33. The United Women's Party (7-90).
34. The Women's Alliance (6-20-91).
35. The Women of Sovereign Russia (7-90).
36. The Russian Communists' Initiative Movement (1990).
37. The Islamic Revival Party (6-9-90).
38. The Committee for Workers' Democracy and Internationalism (1990).
39. The Communist (Neo-Approach) Party of Labor (3-31-89).
40. The Congress of Civil and Patriotic Forces (2-8-91).
41. The Conservative Party (8-5-89).
42. The Constitutional-Democratic Party—The People's Freedom Party (6-91).
43. The Confederation of Labor (5-3-90).
44. The Peasants' Party (9-4-90).
45. The Left-Wing Centrist Bloc (8-1-90).
46. The Liberal-Democratic Party of the Soviet Union (3-31-90).
47. The Liberal Forum (10-2-90).

48. The Libertine Party (5-90).
49. The League of Green Parties (10-26-91).
50. Marxist Workers' Party—The Party of the Dictatorship of the Proletariat (3-24-90).
51. Moscow Young Liberal Union (10-10-90).
52. The Free Russia People's Party (10-26-91).
53. People's Party of Russia (3-10-91).
54. People's Constitutional Party (8-30-90).
55. Popular Orthodox Church Movement (2-22-90).
56. People's Party of Russia (5-19-91). Different from #53.
57. People's Patriotic Party of Russia (2-22-92).
58. People's Labor Union of Russian Solidarity (7-30).
59. Popular Front of the Russian Federation (10-21-89).
60. National League (8-21-90).
61. National Democratic Party (7-89).
62. National-Republican Bloc (11-24-90).
63. National-Social Union (2-24-91).
64. Bloc of Parties New Russia (n.d.).
65. United Front of the Working People (7-15-89).
66. Fatherland (12-20-86).
67. Pamyat (3-91).
68. The Party of Urban and Rural Owners (10-10-88).
69. Green Party (12-88).
70. Party of Constitutional Democrats (1-89).
71. Party of Peace (4-27-90).
72. Party of Free Labor (12-8-90).
73. Party of Socialist Choice and Communist Perspective (10-10-91).
74. Party of Justice (12-6-91).
75. Party of Labor (n.d.).
76. Party of Man (5-11-90).
77. Party of Economic Freedom (n.d.).
78. Rightist-Conservative Movement (10-90).
79. Orthodox Church Monarchist Accord (7-25-90).
80. Orthodox Church Monarchist Order Union (n.d.).
81. Progressive Party of Russia (12-15-90).
82. Workers' Party (2-15-92).
83. Workers' and Peasants' Socialist Party (12-91).

84. Workers' Party of the Dictatorship of the Proletariat (9-14-90).
85. Radical Unifying Association for Peace and Freedom (5-89).
86. Republican Humanitarian Party (11-26-91).
87. Republican Party of Russia (9-90).
88. Republican Party of the Russian Federation (11-17-90).
89. Russian Bourgeois-Democratic Party (7-14-91).
90. Russian Movement for Self-Preservation of Peoples (1-27-92).
91. Russian Democratic Party (n.d.).
92. Russian Movement for Democratic Reforms (2-15-92).
93. Russian Communist Workers' Party (11-24-91).
94. Russian All-People's Union (12-12-91).
95. Russian Party of Democratic Transformations (2-1-92).
96. Russian Green Party (5-27-91).
97. Russian Party of Communists (12-17-91).
98. Russian Party of National Revival (10-16-91).
99. Russian Liberal-Democratic Party (10-6-90).
100. Russian National Party (7-90).
101. Russian National Monarchist Party (5-91).
102. Russian Party of Communists (12-16-91).
103. Russian Party of Leftist Socialist-Oriented Organisations (10-2-91).
104. Russian Christian-Democratic Party (5-12-90).
105. Russian Imperial Union Order (5-90).
106. The Russian People's Assembly (2-9-92).
107. The Russian Democratic Forum (1990).
108. The Russian Christian Democratic Movement (2-90).
109. The Russian Assembly (2-15-92).
110. Russia (6-90).
111. Russian National Unity (9-90).
112. Free Russia (9-89).
113. The Free-Democratic Party of Russia (5-26-90).
114. Slavonic Assembly (12-90).
115. Council of Opposition Movements (3-12-92).
116. Solidarity of Sovereign Republics and Autonomies (11-91).
117. The Social Democratic Workers' Party (2-5-92).
118. The Socialist Party (6-21-90).
119. The Socialist Party of the Working People (12-21-91).

120. The Social-Democratic Party of the Russian Federation (5-4-90).
121. Soyuz ("Union") (12-1-90).
122. The Union of Anarchists (5-9-90).
123. The Union of Non-Party People for Social Justice (1-30-92).
124. Venedi Union (5-90).
125. The Union of Russia' Revival (3-17-90).
126. The Sakharov Union of Democratic Forces (2-3-90).
127. Fatherland Spiritual Regeneration Union (3-16-89).
128. The Modern Marxist Thought Union (2-3-92).
129. The Union of Social Protection of Military Men, Those Liable to Military Service, and Members of Their Families (3-29-89).
130. The Young Russia Union (n.d.).
131. The Christian Regeneration Union (12-17-88).
132. Association of Socialists-Populists (4-90).
133. The Transnational Radical Party (5-3-89).
134. The Working Moscow (n.d.).
135. The Participants of All Wars (10-8-91).
136. The Christian-Democratic Union of Russia (8-4-89).
137. The Christian-Patriotic Union (12-17-88).
138. The Centrist Bloc (2-16-91).
139. The Centrist Bloc of Moderate-Radical Parties and Movements (n.d.).
140. Nuclear Security (12-30-91).

APPENDIX C

Christian Organizations
in Eastern Europe
and the Former Soviet Union

People interested in helping the former Soviet Union should obtain the indispensable *East-West Christian Organizations; A Directory of Western Christian Organizations Working in East Central Europe and the Former Soviet Union,* edited by Sharon Linzey, M. Holt Ruffin, and Mark R. Elliott. The *Directory* is available from the Institute for East-West Christian Studies, Wheaton College, Wheaton, IL 60187, (708) 752-5917.

The so-called Draft Edition of the *Directory* released in May 1992 (114 pages) lists and describes 330 organizations, although the database from which the list was developed documents over 800 organizations. A completed and comprehensive *Directory* detailing all 800 organizations was due for release late in 1992. The *Directory's* alphabetical list includes, for each organization, its chief executive officer, geographical area of ministry, type of work, general description, denominational affiliation, address, and phone number. It classifies twelve types of church and parachurch outreach:

1. Arts
2. Bible study programs
3. Donations of funds and equipment

4. Evangelism and church planting
5. Family ministries and social services
6. Leadership training, aid to seminaries
7. Media (television, radio, video)
8. Medicines and medical care
9. Military chaplaincies
10. Prison ministries
11. Publications, such as Bibles and children's literature
12. Youth work, such as summer camps and sports

A second phase of the project has now begun that will document the *indigenous* church and parachurch organizations working in Eastern Europe and the former Soviet Union, forming a parallel *Directory* to supplement the present one. Sharon Linzey will direct this second phase of the project from Moscow, in connection with the International Institute for Christian Studies (Overland Park, KS 66282-2147) and the Institute for East-West Christian Studies (Wheaton, IL 60187).

Select Bibliography

Alexeev, Wasslij, and Theofanis Stavrou. *The Great Revival: The Russian Church under German Occupation*. Minneapolis: Burgess, 1976.

Anderson, Paul B. *People, Church and State in Modern Russia*. Westport, Conn.: Hyperion, 1981.

Aslund, Anders. *Gorbachev's Struggle for Economic Reform*. Ithaca, N.Y.: Cornell University Press, 1989.

Beeson, Trevor. *Discretion and Valour: Religious Conditions in Russia and Eastern Europe*. Rev. ed. London: Collins, 1982.

Bennigsen, Alexandre. "Islam in the USSR." *Soviet Jewish Affairs* 2 (1979).

Benz, E. *The Eastern Orthodox Church*. New York: Doubleday, Anchor Books, 1963.

Berdyaev, Nicolas. *The Beginning and the End*. New York: Harper, 1957.

———. *The Origin of Russian Communism*. Ann Arbor, Mich.: University of Michigan Press, 1991.

———. *The Russian Idea*. Boston: Beacon, 1962.

Bialer, Seweryn, ed. *Inside Gorbachev's Russia*. Boulder, Colo.: Westview, 1989.

Billington, James H. *The Icon and the Axe: An Interpretive History of Russian Culture*. New York: Vintage, 1970.

Bociurkiw, Bohdan R. *Ukrainian Churches under Soviet Rule: Two Case Studies*. Cambridge: Harvard University Ukrainian Studies Fund, 1984.

Bociurkiw, Bohdan R., and J. Strong, eds. *Religion and Atheism in the USSR and Eastern Europe*. Toronto: University Press, 1975.

Bockmuehl, Klaus. *The Challenge of Marxism.* Colorado Springs, Colo.: Helmers and Howard, 1986.

Boiter, Albert. *Religion in the Soviet Union.* Washington, D.C.: Center for Strategic and International Studies, 1980.

Bourdeaux, Lorna, and Michael Bordeaux. *Ten Growing Soviet Churches.* Bromley, Kent (Great Britain): MARC Europe, 1987.

Bourdeaux, Michael. *Gorbachev, Glasnost, and the Gospel.* London: Hodder and Stoughton, 1990.

———. *Patriarch and Prophets: Persecution of the Russian Orthodox Church.* London: Mowbrays, 1975.

———. *Religious Ferment in Russia: Protestant Opposition to Soviet Religious Policy.* London: Macmillan, 1968.

———. *Risen Indeed: Lessons in Faith from the USSR.* Crestwood, N.Y.: St. Vladimir's Seminary Press, 1983.

Brzezinski, Zbigniew. *The Grand Failure.* New York: Charles Scribner's Sons, 1989.

Bulgakov, Sergei. *The Orthodox Church.* Crestwood, N.Y.: St. Vladimir's Seminary Press, 1988.

Buss, Gerald. *The Bear's Hug: Christian Belief and the Soviet State, 1917–1968.* Grand Rapids: Eerdmans, 1987.

Calian, Carnegie S. *Theology Without Boundaries: Encounters of Eastern Orthodoxy and Western Tradition.* Louisville: West/John Knox, 1992.

———. *Icon and Pulpit: The Protestant-Orthodox Encounter.* Philadelphia: Westminster, 1968.

Chamberlain, William H. *The Russian Revolution, 1917–1921.* 2 vols. New York, 1965.

Chmykhalov, Timothy. *The Last Christian: The Release of the Siberian Seven.* Grand Rapids: Zondervan, 1986.

Cohen, Stephen. *Rethinking the Soviet Experience.* New York: Oxford University Press, 1989.

Cohen, Stephen F., and Katrina vanden Heuvel. *Voices of Glasnost.* New York: W. W. Norton, 1989.

Conquest, Robert. *The Great Terror: Stalin's Purge of the 1930s.* Rev. ed. Oxford: Oxford University Press, 1990.

———. *The Harvest of Sorrows: Soviet Collectivization and the Terror-Famine.* Oxford: Oxford University Press, 1986.

———. *The Last Empire: Nationality and the Soviet Future.* Stanford, Calif.: Hoover Institution Press, 1986.

———. *Religion in the USSR*. New York: Praeger, 1968.

Coplestone, Frederick C. *Philosophy in Russia: From Herzen to Lenin and Berdyaev*. Notre Dame, Ind.: University of Notre Dame Press, 1986.

———. *Russian Religious Philosophy: Selected Aspects*. Notre Dame, Ind.: University of Notre Dame Press, 1988.

Curtiss, John Shelton. *Church and State in Russia, 1900–1917*. New York: Octagon, 1940.

———. *The Russian Church and the Soviet State, 1917–1950*. Boston: Little, Brown, 1953.

Czesniak, Boleslaw, ed. *The Russian Revolution and Religion*. Notre Dame, Ind.: University of Notre Dame Press, 1959.

Dudko, Dmitri. *Our Hope*. Crestwood, N.Y.: St. Vladimir's Seminary Press, 1977.

Durasoff, Steve. *Pentecost behind the Iron Curtain*. Plainfield, N.J.: Logos International, 1972.

———. *The Russian Protestants: Evangelicals in the Soviet Union, 1944–1964*. Madison, N.J.: Farleigh-Dickinson University Press, 1969.

Dvornik, F. *Byzantium and the Roman Primacy*. New York: Fordham University Press, 1966.

Elliott, Mark, ed. *Christianity and Marxism Worldwide: An Annotated Bibliography*. Wheaton, Ill.: Institute for the Study of Christianity and Marxism, 1989.

———, ed. *East European Missions Directory*. Wheaton, Ill.: Institute for the Study of Christianity and Marxism, 1989.

Ellis, Jane. *The Russian Orthodox Church: A Contemporary History*. Bloomington, Ind.: Indiana University Press, 1986.

Evdokimov, P. *L'Orthodoxie*. Paris, 1959.

Fedotov, George. *The Russian Religious Mind*. New York: Harper Torchbooks, 1965.

———. *A Treasury of Russian Spirituality*. London, 1950.

Fletcher, William C. *Religion and Soviet Foreign Policy*. London: Oxford University Press, 1973.

———. *The Russian Orthodox Church Underground, 1917–1970*. London: Oxford University Press, 1971.

———. *Soviet Believers: The Religious Sector of the Population*. Lawrence, Kans.: Regents Press of Kansas, 1981.

———. *Soviet Charismatics*. New York: Peter Lang, 1985.

———. *A Study in Survival: The Church in Russia, 1927–1943.* New York: Macmillan, 1965.

Florovsky, G. *The Collected Works.* 10 volumes. Cambridge, Mass.: Nordland, 1972–1987.

———. *Ways of Russian Theology.* Paris: YMCA, 1981.

Forest, Jim. *Pilgrim to the Russian Church.* New York: Crossroad, 1988.

Gilboa, Yehoshua. *The Black Years of Soviet Jewery, 1939–1953.* Boston, 1971.

Gillquist, Peter E. *Becoming Orthodox: A Journey to the Ancient Christian Faith.* Brentwood, Tenn.: Wolgemuth and Hyatt, 1989.

———. *Making America Orthodox.* Brookline, Mass.: Holy Cross Orthodox Press, 1984.

Gorbachev, Mikhail. *The August Coup.* San Francisco: HarperCollins, 1991.

———. *Perestroika: New Thinking for Our Country and the World.* New York: Harper and Row, 1988.

Handbook for Christian Travelers to the USSR (anonymous). Wheaton, Ill.: Slavic Gospel Association, 1991.

Hebly, Hans. *Protestants in Russia.* Belfast: Christian Journals, 1976.

Heller, Mikhail, and Aleksandr M. Nekrich. *Utopia in Power: The History of the Soviet Union from 1917 to the Present.* New York: Summit, 1986.

Hill, Kent R. *The Soviet Union on the Brink: An Inside Look at Christianity and Glasnost.* Portland: Multnomah, 1991.

———. *Turbulent Times for the Soviet Church.* Portland: Multnomah, 1991.

Hopko, Thomas. *All The Fullness of God: Essays on Orthodoxy, Ecumenism, and Modern Society.* Crestwood, N.Y.: St. Vladimir's Seminary Press, 1982.

———. *The Lenten Spring: Readings for Great Lent.* Crestwood, N.Y.: St. Vladimir's Seminary Press, 1983.

———. *The Orthodox Faith.* 4 vols. Crestwood, N.Y.: St. Vladimir's Seminary Press, 1984.

———. *The Winter Pascha: Readings for the Christmas-Epiphany Season.* Crestwood, N.Y.: St. Vladimir's Seminary Press, 1984.

———. *Women and the Priesthood.* Crestwood, N.Y.: St. Vladimir's Seminary Press, n.d.

Hosking, Geoffrey. *The Awakening of the Soviet Union.* Cambridge, Mass.: Harvard University Press, 1990.

House, Francis. *Millennium of Faith: Christianity in Russia, 988–1988 AD.* Crestwood, N.Y.: St. Vladimir's Seminary Press, 1988.

Kline, George. *Religions and Anti-Religious Thought in Russia*. Chicago: University of Chicago Press, 1968.

Lane, Christel. *Christian Religion in the Soviet Union: A Sociological Study*. Boston: Allen and Unwin, 1978.

Lossky, Vladimir. *In the Image and Likeness of God*. Crestwood, N.Y.: St. Vladimir's Seminary Press, 1974.

———. *The Mystical Theology of the Orthodox Church*. Crestwood, N.Y.: St. Vladimir's Seminary Press, 1986.

———. *Orthodox Theology: An Introduction*. New York, 1978.

———. *The Vision of God*. London, 1963.

Maksudov, M. "Losses Suffered by the Population of the USSR, 1918–1958." *Samizdat Register II*. New York, 1981.

Maloney, George. *A History of Orthodox Theology Since 1453*. Belmont, Mass.: Nordland, 1973.

Marshall, Richard. *Aspects of Religion in the Soviet Union, 1917–1967*. Chicago: University of Chicago Press, 1971.

Medish, Vadim. *The Soviet Union*. 4th ed. Englewood Cliffs, N.J.: Prentice-Hall, 1991.

Medvedev, Roy. *Let History Judge: The Origins and Consequences of Stalinism*. Rev. ed. New York: Columbia University Press, 1989.

———. *On Stalin and Stalinism*. Oxford: Oxford University Press, 1973.

Meyendorff, John. *The Byzantine Legacy in the Orthodox Church*. Crestwood, N.Y.: St. Vladimir's Seminary Press, 1982.

———. *Byzantine Theology: Historical Trends and Doctrinal Themes*. New York, 1974.

———. *Christ in Eastern Orthodox Thought*. Crestwood, N.Y.: St. Vladimir's Seminary Press, 1975.

———. *Living Tradition*. Crestwood, N.Y.: St. Vladimir's Seminary Press, 1978.

Meyendorf, John and Joseph McLelland, eds. *The New Man: An Orthodox and Reformed Dialogue*. New Brunswick, N.J.: Standard Press for Agora Books, 1973.

———. *The Orthodox Church*. 2d ed. Crestwood, N.Y.: St. Vladimir's Seminary Press, 1981.

———. *Orthodoxy and Catholicity*. New York, 1966.

———. *St. Gregory Palamas and Orthodox Spirituality*. Crestwood, N.Y.: St. Vladimir's Seminary Press, 1974.

Morrison, Donald, ed. *Mikhail S. Gorbachev: An Intimate Biography.* New York: Time, 1988.

Nahaylo, Bogdan, and Victor Swoboda. *Soviet Disunion: A History of the Nationalities Problem in the USSR.* New York: Free, 1990.

Nesdoly, Samuel. *Among the Soviet Evangelicals.* Carlisle, Pa.: Banner of Truth, 1986.

Nichols, Robert, and Theofanis Stavrou. *Russian Orthodoxy under the Old Regime.* Minneapolis: University of Minnesota Press, 1978.

Niesel, Wilhelm. *Reformed Symbolics: A Comparison of Catholicism, Orthodoxy, and Protestantism.* N.P.: Oliver and Boyd, 1962.

Nove, Alec. *An Economic History of the USSR.* Rev. ed. Middlesex, England: Penguin, 1982.

O'Callaghan, Paul. *An Eastern Orthodox Response to Evangelical Claims.* Minneapolis: Light and Life Publishers, 1984.

Oden, Thomas. *Two Worlds: Notes on the Death of Modernity in America and Russia.* Downers Grove, Ill.: InterVarsity, 1992.

Ouspensky, L. *Theology of the Icon.* New York, 1978.

Ouspensky, L., and V. Lossky. *The Meaning of Icons.* Olten, 1952.

Pain, James, and Nicholas Zernov, eds. *A Bulgakov Anthology.* Philadelphia: Westminster, 1976.

Pelikan, Jaroslav. *The Spirit of Eastern Christendom (600–1700).* Chicago: University of Chicago Press, 1974.

Petro, Nicolai N., ed. *Christianity and Russian Culture in Soviet Society.* Boulder, Colo.: Westview, 1990.

Pollock, John C. *The Faith of Russian Evangelicals.* New York: McGraw-Hill, 1964.

———. *The Siberian Seven.* Waco, Tex.: Word, 1979.

Pospielovsky, Dmitry. *A History of Marxist-Leninist Atheism and Soviet Anti-religious Policies.* 3 vols. New York: St. Martin's, 1987–88.

———. *The Russian Church under the Soviet Regime, 1917–1982.* 2 vols. Crestwood, N.Y.: St. Vladimir's Seminary Press, 1984.

Powell, David E. *Antireligious Propaganda in the Soviet Union.* Cambridge, Mass.: MIT, 1975.

Pushkarev, Sergei, et al. *Christianity and Government in Russia and the Soviet Union: Reflections on the Millennium.* Boulder, Colo.: Westview, 1989.

Quenot, Michel. *The Icon.* Crestwood, N.Y.: SUSP, 1991.

Ramet, Pedro. *Cross and Commissar: The Politics of Religion in Eastern Europe and the USSR*. Bloomington, Ind.: Indiana University Press, 1987.

Reimer, Johannes. *Operation Soviet Union: How to Pray for the 160 People Groups in the USSR*. Fresno, Calif.: Logos, 1990.

Sakharov, Andrei. "A Letter from Exile." *New York Times Magazine,* June 8, 1980.

———. *My Country and the World*. New York, 1975.

Sawatsky, Walter. *Soviet Evangelicals since World War II*. Scottdale, Pa.: Herald, 1981.

Scheffbusch, Winrich. *Christians under the Hammer and Sickle*. Grand Rapids: Zondervan, 1974.

Schmemann, A. *An Introduction to Liturgical Theology*. Crestwood, N.Y.: St. Vladimir's Seminary Press, 1986.

———. *The Eucharist*. Crestwood, N.Y.: St. Vladimir's Seminary Press, 1988.

———. *For the Life of the World: The Sacraments and Orthodoxy*. Crestwood, N.Y.: St. Vladimir's Seminary Press, 1973.

———. *The Historical Road of Eastern Orthodoxy*. New York, 1973.

———. *Ultimate Questions: An Anthology of Modern Russian Religious Thought*. Crestwood, N.Y.: St. Vladimir's Seminary Press, 1965.

Shelton, Judy. *The Coming of the Soviet Crash*. New York: Free, 1989.

Simis, Konstantin. *USSR: The Corrupt Society*. New York: Simon and Schuster, 1982.

Simon, Gerhard. *Church, State, and Opposition in the USSR*. London: C. Hurst, 1974.

Smith, Hedrick. *The Russians*. Rev. ed. New York: Ballantine, 1984.

———. *The New Russians*. New York: Random House, 1990.

Solzhenitsyn, Alexander. *The Gulag Archipelago, 1918–1956*. New York: Harper and Row, 1985.

———. *Letter to Soviet Leaders*. New York: Harper and Row, 1975.

———. *One Day in the Life of Ivan Denisovich*. New York: Bantam, 1976.

Spinka, Matthew. *The Church and the Russian Revolution*. New York: Macmillan, 1927.

———. *The Church in Soviet Russia*. Westport, Conn.: Greenwood, 1980.

Stroyen, W. B. *Communist Russia and the Russian Orthodox Church, 1943–1962*. Washington, D.C.: Catholic University of America Press, 1967.

Struve, Nikita. *Christians in Contemporary Russia*. London, 1967.

Suziedelis, Saulius. *The Sword and the Cross: A History of the Church in Lithuania*. Huntington, Ind.: Our Sunday Visitor, 1988.

Szczesniak, Boleslaw, ed. *The Russian Revolution and Religion: A Collection of Documents Concerning the Supression of Religion by the Communists, 1917–1925*. Notre Dame: University of Notre Dame Press, 1959.

Tobia, Robert, and John Meyendorf, eds. *Salvation in Christ: Lutheran-Orthodox Dialogue*. Either Augsburg or Fortress, 1992.

Thrower, James. *Marxist-Leninist "Scientific Atheism" and the Study of Religion and Atheism in the USSR*. New York: Mouton, 1983.

Tucker, Robert. "The Rise of Stalin's Personality Cult." *American Historical Review* 84/2 (1979).

———, ed. *Stalinism: Essays in Historical Interpretation*. New York, 1977.

Tumarkin, Nina. *Lenin Lives! The Lenin Cult in Soviet Russia*. Cambridge, Mass.: Harvard University Press, 1983.

Vgolnik, Anthony. *The Illuminating Icon*. Grand Rapids: Eerdmans, 1989.

Vardys, V. Stanley. *The Catholic Church, Dissent, and Nationality in Soviet Lithuania*. Boulder, 1978.

Voobus, Arthur. *The Martyrs of Estonia: The Suffering, Ordeal, and Annihilation of the Churches under the Russian Occupation*. Stockholm: Estonian Evangelical Lutheran Church, 1984.

Walker, Martin. *Waking Giant: Gorbachev's Russia*. New York: Pantheon, 1987.

Walsh, David. *After Ideology: Recovering the Spiritual Foundations of Freedom*. San Francisco: HarperCollins, 1990.

Ware, Timothy. *The Orthodox Church*. New York: Penguin, 1964.

Weiant, E. T. "Sources of Mass Atheism in Russia" (Ph.D. diss., Basel, 1950).

Yancey, Philip. *Praying with the KGB: A Startling Report From a Shattered Empire*. Portland: Multnomah, 1992.

Yeltsin, Boris. *Against the Grain*. New York: Summit, 1990.

Zatko, James. *Descent into Hell: The Destruction of the Roman Catholic Church in Russia, 1917–1923*. Notre Dame, Ind.: University of Notre Dame Press, 1965.

Zernov, Nicholas. *Moscow the Third Rome*. London, 1937.

———. *The Russian Religious Renaissance of the Twentieth Century*. London: Darton, Longman, and Todd, 1963.

———. *The Russians and Their Church*. London, 1945.

Index